THE TRUE PATH,

OR THE

YOUNG MAN INVITED TO THE SAVIOUR.

IN A SERIES OF LECTURES.

BY THE

REV. JOSEPH M. ATKINSON.

RALEIGH, N. C.

PHILADELPHIA:

PRESBYTERIAN BOARD OF PUBLICATION,

No. 821 CHESTNUT STREET.

STEREOTYPED BY WILLIAM W. HARDING PHILADELPHIA.

Remember now thy Creator in the days of thy youth, while the evil days come not, nor the years draw nigh, when thou shalt say, I have no pleasure in them. Ecc. xii. 1.

And the king said, Is the young man safe? 2 Sam. xviii. 29.

Wherewith shall a young man cleanse his way? By taking heed thereto according to thy word. Ps. cxix. 9.

Run and speak to that young man. Zech. ii. 4.

Thy creatures have been my books, but thy Scriptures much more. I have sought thee in the courts, fields, and gardens, but I have found thee in thy temples.—LORD BACON.

The end of learning is to repair the ruins of our first parents, by regaining to know God aright, and out of that knowledge to love him, to imitate him, to be like him, as we may the nearest, by possessing our souls of true virtue, which, being united to the heavenly grace of faith, makes up the highest perfection.—JOHN MILTON.

That religion must needs be worth looking into, which so many wise and excellent men do so much value above their lives and fortunes.—JEREMY TAYLOR.

TO

REV. JOHN M. P. ATKINSON, D. D.,

PRESIDENT OF HAMPDEN SIDNEY COLLEGE, VA.

THE FACT, THAT YOU HAVE BEEN CALLED IN THE PROVIDENCE OF GOD, TO PRESIDE OVER THE INTERESTS AND DESTINIES OF ONE OF THE MOST ANCIENT AND NOT THE LEAST HONOURED AND USEFUL OF THE COLLEGES OF OUR NATIVE STATE, WOULD SEEM TO RENDER THE DEDICATION OF THIS VOLUME TO YOU, A THING NOT LESS PROPER IN ITSELF, THAN GRATEFUL TO MY OWN FEELINGS.

CONTENTS.

LECTURE VIII.

LECTURE IX.

LECTURE X.

LECTURE XI.

LECTURE XII.

LECTURE XIII.

LECTURE XIV.

PREFACE.

THE rapid multiplication of Young Men's Christian Associations is a noticeable fact of the age. It at once indicates a disease, and furnishes at least a partial remedy. The disease is the unnatural and perilous aggregation of young men in cities and villages in which the temptations to extravagance, dissipation, and vice peculiarly abound; and in which the restraining and meliorating influences of domestic life are in many instances wholly unknown. The remedy is a counter-movement of Christian benevolence, which seeks out such—throws around them the guards of sympathy and virtue; leads them to the sanctuary of God; and gives them access to select periodicals, books, and newspapers.

The happy influence of such associations, when rightly constituted and conducted, and rigidly confined to their proper sphere, can hardly be over-estimated; and it is with a view to their special needs and uses, that this book has been prepared.

I have aimed to adapt it to them, and to young men of whom the number is very great and perpetually increasing, who are pursuing a course of liberal study in high schools, academies, and colleges.

In its style and structure, I have endeavoured to make it attractive to cultivated young men; and at the same time, render it intelligible to those who have never been much conversant with moral and metaphysical enquiries.

The staple of the book is the doctrines of Evangelical Protestant Theology, as opposed to the perversions of Popery on the one side, and the negations and errors of Rationalistic infidelity on the other.

There are few, if any, detailed discussions of particular vices, not only because such discussions are found in sufficient plenty elsewhere—in Sermons and Lectures addressed to young men—but because my endeavour has been to develope, and inculcate principles, which, cordially adopted and acted on, would cut off all particular vices; implant and nourish all particular virtues. General principles bear the same relation to particular precepts, which Algebra bears to Arithmetic; the formula applied in the solution of a particular problem, embracing any number of problems of like conditions.

I am persuaded that the body of virtue is one, and the life of virtue one; that all particular virtues flow from the one comprehensive principle of obedience to God, founded on love; and that the avoidance of all particular vices flows from the operation of the fear of God, founded on faith, fixed in the heart and ruling the life with imperial sway.

I have endeavoured, so far as it extends, to make it such a book, as I now feel would have been useful to me when a young man in college; and such a book as a Christian parent might put into the hands of a son, not only with confidence that its teachings were scriptural, but with the hope that, with the blessing of God, they might be saving. If it shall be the means of confirming any young disciple in "the faith once delivered;" or in rescuing any from the deadly delusions of prevalent forms of infidelity, I shall have abundant cause for thanksgiving in the attainment of the end for which it was written.

THE TRUE PATH,

OR THE

YOUNG MAN INVITED TO THE SAVIOUR.

LECTURE I.

INTRODUCTORY — DIVINE REVELATION — GENERAL STATEMENT OF ITS CLAIMS AND ASPECTS.

GOD has graciously revealed all necessary truth, in the gospel of his Son. He has fully unfolded a costly and magnificent scheme of redemption, in which his own glory and the salvation of the believer, are identified and secured. The Lord Jesus Christ as the Author and the Finisher of our faith, with obedience as its test, holiness as its fruit, and salvation as its end, is offered to all men on every page. The wickedness and folly of those who refuse and rebel, are condemned in the strongest terms. Total indifference, the most unreasonable, the most common, and the most fatal species of infatuation, is made matter of particular mention and vehement rebuke. Speaking by the mouth of the wisest of men, he says: "To you, O men, I call; and my voice is to the sons of men. Hear, for I will speak of excellent things, and the opening of my mouth shall be right things." Prov. viii. 4, 6. Seeming even to mourn over the obstinate disobedience of his chosen people, he addresses them by the lips of Isaiah, in these singular terms, "Oh! that thou hadst hearkened to my commandments! then had thy peace been as a river, and thy righteousness as the waves of the sea." Isaiah xlviii. 18.

Inattention to the paramount claims of divine revelation may be traced ultimately to a wilful and guilty ignorance. The transcendent importance of the subject; the everlasting issues depending on a right decision; the favourable verdict of the most powerful and independent minds that have yet arisen among the most enlightened nations; the willing homage of Bacon, Milton, Newton, Locke, and Boyle, to the solid foundation of its claims, have not been sufficient to arrest the anxious attention of the larger portion of mankind.

The more profound our examination, and the more extended our knowledge of the system of Religion revealed in the Bible, the more assured will be our conviction that it came from God ; and that it has divine power to enlighten, to console, to sanctify, and to save. Systems of man's device may be exposed by an intelligent and thorough scrutiny; but that plan of salvation which descended from heaven, and is recorded in the book of God, has nothing to dread from the most searching examination.

Excluding, for a moment, the retributions of eternity, and regarding only its historical influence and the magnitude of its claims, this system deserves the attention of wise and thoughtful men. Its enemies themselves being judges, it is a powerful agent and has effected immense results. It has not failed to mould the character of every people, among whom it has obtained a transient footing, even in a corrupted form. It has given tone to the laws, to the civil institutions, and to the social usages of every civilized state. The code of Moses has formed the basis of the code of Christendom, and especially of the legal system which prevails in this country and in Great Britain, the foremost nations in all the world, in the elements and the fruits of moral greatness.

From the period of its first appearance, it has been charged, and not unjustly, with being exclusive. It cannot, like the tolerant and easy systems of Paganism, bear a competitor. Wherever it prevails, and just so far as it prevails, every idolatrous rival must be thrown to the moles and to the bats. Not content with setting forth its own claims to the belief and obedience of mankind, it denounces every other system of salvation as delusive, and proclaims every other god, than Jehovah, false. In this the New Testament is not less uncompromising than the Old. It says, "If any man love not the Lord

Jesus Christ, let him be Anathema, Maranatha;" 1 Cor. xvi. 22; that "there is none other name under heaven given among men whereby we must be saved;" Acts iv. 12; that every other refuge is a refuge of lies, which will be swept away when He shall rise up in the fierceness of his wrath, and be destroyed with the brightness of his coming. It aims at nothing less than setting up an interior dominion in the heart of man; bringing every thought into captivity to the obedience of Christ; planting an incorruptible seed in the soul, which is constantly to grow in power, until finally it shall pervade and sanctify every faculty; yielding precious fruits: holiness in life; peace in death; and happiness in heaven. No sovereignty ever known among men by the articulate confession of one of the very greatest of earthly sovereigns—Napoleon—can be compared either in the completeness or in the permanence of its sway with that kingdom which its divine Founder declared not to be of this world.

That which gives coherence, clearness, and completeness to the whole Bible—to the Old Testament not less than to the New; and binds the whole together with the golden chain of unity, is the marvellous testimony which it delivers in type and symbol—in prophecy and history—to the person, work, and grace of the Lord Jesus Christ, Immanuel, God manifest in the flesh for our salvation. Strike Christ from the Bible and it is like striking the sun from our system; all is darkness and confusion; the vacuity and emptiness of the original chaos! As formed in the heart of the believer, he is the hope of glory; as in the infinite effulgence of his exalted person, he is the light of the heavenly temple; so the revealed Redeemer of God's elect is the sun of the inspired Scriptures. The facts connected with him render the doctrines and declarations of the whole Bible, clear and harmonious; hence it happens that they who deny his divine claims, and degrade his divine person, are inevitably forced to deny other truths, and often lapse by degrees into the fathomless abyss of Atheism. The only schemes of theology self-consistent throughout are evangelical christianity at the one pole, and absolute atheism at the other. Every intermediate system is a compromise and a contradiction.

The one great fact to which all the Apostles bear witness with united voice is, that Jesus Christ came into the world to save sinners; that he "who being in the form of God, thought it not robbery to be equal with God, made himself of no reputation, and took upon him the form of a servant, and was made in the likeness of men; and being found in fashion as a man, humbled himself and became obedient unto death, even the death of the cross." Phil. ii. 6-8. This is in brief, the sum of their testimony. To this they were divinely constituted witnesses. And if the ministers of Christ now would have the same success, they must bear a faithful testimony to the same truth. The great doctrines of atonement by the precious blood of the Lamb of God; and justification by faith in his name, must be not obscurely recognized in their preaching, nor remotely inferred from it, but plainly and prominently set forth. Their inseparable connection with the honour of God, with the satisfaction of law, and with the peace of the believer, must be made to appear.

The church of the living God is the woman of the Apocalypse—the woman clothed with the sun. Rev. xii. 1. The servant of Christ, therefore, should take his stand in the very centre of the Gospel system—the focal point of its peculiar glory. The light of the knowledge of the glory of God, as it shines in the face of Jesus Christ, should be seen to shine in him with a lustre limited indeed by the finite capacities of man, but pure as when it sprang from the bosom of the infinite God. The law of the Lord should dwell upon his lips; the gentleness of heaven in his heart and on his brow. He should build his argument on the immovable basis of the love of God, revealed in redemption. He should draw his exhortations to obedience from the example of Jesus, and his incitements to devotion, from the solitude of the mountain and the fervours of his midnight prayer.

No inferior motive—no meaner topic should be permitted to usurp the place of these. May he not without presumption hope to convince, to warn, to counsel and to comfort, whose arguments rest on God; whose warnings are drawn from the interminable agonies of hell; whose counsels are dictated by the inspiration of the Almighty; and whose comfort is supplied by the Holy Ghost? The glorious *shekinah* of God, the appointed symbol of the divine Majesty, rested on the mercy-seat; thus foreshadowing mercy and truth met together, righteousness and peace embracing each other. Above shone the holiness of God in all its inaccessible and intolerable brightness; and underneath was placed the ample basis of peace and pardon. Thus does the Lord our righteousness fulfil the law and propitiate the "holiness of God," at the very moment that he gives the largest scope to mercy and grace. The work of redemption by Christ Jesus is a work every way worthy of God. It is a work which it required the love of God to originate; John iii. 16; the wisdom of God to devise; the power of God to execute; and the grace of God to apply. The recognition of Christ is, therefore, an infallible test of the true relation of the soul to God and to the gospel salvation. The due apprehension of spiritual things is just in proportion as they are spiritual; the most purely and highly spiritual demanding the clearest and nicest perception, and appealing to the deepest and most delicate sympathies. Therefore the Lord Jesus being in his person the fountain of spiritual life; in his doctrine the sum of spiritual truth; and in his character the standard of spiritual beauty; the right apprehension of Christ may be regarded as the measure of our illumination and the test of our moral excellence. Hence the question, "What think ye of Christ?" is reckoned, in the Scripture, so decisive of our standing in the sight of God and of our destiny for ever. The faculty of discovering Christ everywhere in the Scriptures in the types and shadows and ceremonies of the law, of which we have such signal instances in Matthew Henry and in Andrew Bonar, and perhaps more remarkably than in either, in the saintly McCheyne—is a token of discriminating wisdom and of delicate spiritual tact. Christ is with us in his providence, when we think not of him. Like the disciples when they saw him walking on the sea, we vaguely discover the outlines of his beloved form, but require the gracious assurance of his compassionate voice, " It is I; be not afraid." Mark vi. 50. So he is with us in the word of his grace, but we perceive him not because our eyes, like those of the disciples, "are holden." The inward unction of the Holy Ghost is essential to a correct apprehension of revealed truth; to a saving knowledge of the incarnate God. For the truth may be clearly discerned by the natural understanding and yet make no impression on the heart; or excite only opposition and disgust. Mixed with faith and impressed by the Holy Spirit, it is not only understood but acquiesced in, and not only acquiesced in but rejoiced in; it is then not better known than loved; the strong affections of the soul keeping pace with the clear apprehensions of the mind. John i.

12; 2 Cor. iv. 13; 1 John iii. 24; John xvi. 13. Hence it is that the saving knowledge of God and of his Christ can never be got by definition or description. It can be attained only by experience; the Holy Ghost himself being the teacher.

As a man with weak or impaired vision can see comparatively little; though all the wonders of earth and sky—of land and sea—be spread out before him; and one with strong and clear vision, can take in a wide and varied prospect of "meadow, grove, and stream;" so it is with the eye of the mind. The material world does not exhibit the same aspects, suggest the same truths, or convey the same lessons to all men indifferently. How much more is suggested to an Aristotle and Bacon; to a Newton, a Franklin, a Humboldt, by the sensible phenomena before us, than to men in general, who pass through the world with their eyes shut or dreaming—rational somnambulists? To the eye of an angel, still more to the eye of the omniscient Creator, there is infinitely more in the universe than the most gifted of the sons of men have been able to see or to divine. So it is in relation to the hidden riches of the word of God. The Bible is not the same book to every reader; just as the visible universe is not the same object to every observer. To perfect knowledge and to perfect enjoyment, it is not less essential that the organ of discernment be clear and sound, than that the object of attention be instructive and beautiful. With many now as with the Jews of old, 2 Cor. iii. 14, there is a veil on the mind in the reading of the Scriptures; which renders it impossible for them to discern their most delicate beauties—or to appreciate their most precious lessons. This veil it is the province of the Holy Spirit to take away; and exhibit the word of God in its unsearchable riches of truth and wisdom, of grace and glory.

The Bible comes to us originally from God; mediately by man. There are accordingly two ways of looking at it. The one is to confine our regards to the human instruments, through whose agency it was given to us. This is the method of the rationalist. The other is to contemplate it as essentially a revelation *from* God and *of* God; inspired by his Spirit, and instinct with his presence. This is the method of the enlightened believer. We may therefore read it grammatically, critically, coldly, intellectually; weighing carefully every sentence and word and syllable and punctuation-point, just as we should read any mere human production. Or we may take it up with the vital interest, with the sacred awe, with the implicit faith, with the humble docility, and with the fervent prayer for the promised teaching of the Holy Ghost, which befit the word of the only wise God, our Father, in the hands of his lowly children. The way to read it to good purpose, is to make every passage our own, by a diligent self-application, whether it be a command, a prohibition, a precept, a promise, or a prayer. So studied, its glorious divinity shines out, as sun-light from the parted cloud; its ineffable sweetness streams out, as the juice from the full and fragrant clusters of the grape; its sovereign majesty is felt, its heavenly grace is tasted, its matchless and mysterious power to subdue, to sanctify, and to cheer the soul, is infallibly evinced. The soul of the believer instinctively moves toward God; strives after communion with him in his word and ordinances, as the flower struggles toward the light. He now feels that one hour's fellowship with the Father, through the gracious mediation of his dear Son, is worth a whole lifetime of sensual bliss; and he anticipates with irrepressible ardour and delight, the spiritual joys of heaven.

The more the Christian reads the Scriptures, and ponders the Scriptures, and prays over the Scriptures, the better will he understand, the more will he revere and love them. Approaching the recorded revelations of God, in this frame of mind, they have for us an indescribable elevation and a peculiar charm. Studied in the spirit in which they were given under His power who indited them—read in the pure light of heaven under which they were written; their superhuman glory will be intuitively, unmistakably, and profoundly apprehended. Thus contemplated, the vast and simple grandeur of Bible revelations, on a general and comprehensive survey, cannot but strike the mind. There is a majestic harmony in all the proportions of Christian truth;

in all the propositions of the Christian theology. As St. Peter's at Rome is said to impress the eye of the beholder with its finished symmetry and proportioned beauty; as the glorious dome of the firmament gives a still higher impression of unity and greatness, so likewise the Bible. There is not a logical merely, but a theological and transcendental relation among the several parts of this spiritual temple of God;—a relation among its several doctrines higher than any formal logic of man's discovery or device; deeper than any analogies or processes of nature; of vast but still measured correspondence between the various but never conflicting truths of divine revelation; the absolute sovereignty of God and the free agency of man; the doctrine of divine election and the doctrine of human responsibility. These several truths elude our grasp and rise above our comprehension, by reason not of their obscurity but of their sublimity. The method of conciliation is unknown to us, not from any want of congruity in them, but from the limited range of our reason. The darkness is all our own, in God is light and in him is no darkness at all. When we come into the world of Scripture we come into a world of wonders. There is the immensity, the variety, the magnificence of nature. Every thing is on a stupendous scale; the holiness and love, the wrath and the mercy of God. Those doctrines of divine revelation which are most offensive to the pride of human reason, and to the corruption of the human heart, rest upon precisely the same *testimony*, with those which are most gladly received; as, for instance, the eternal punishment of the wicked in a future state of existence, and the everlasting blessedness of the righteous. Matt. xxv. 46. All the truths of divine revelation relating directly to God and to the destiny of the human soul, have an immeasurable significance and grandeur. When we think therefore, of the catastrophe impending over the impenitent sinner, let us not lose sight of the associated truths—the inconceivable height of heavenly glory to which the believer is advanced; the ample provision made for our salvation in the redemption by Christ Jesus; the transcendent wisdom and excellence of the law violated; the infinite elevation of the Being affronted; the unutterable majesty and merit of the Son of God who died for our sins according to the Scriptures.

In its lowest function, as a means of intellectual culture, as a gymnastic of the mind, indispensable to its fullest and finest development, the Bible is worthy of all study and of all praise. Some classes of books are positively pernicious to some classes of minds; as poetry and fiction to excessively ardent and imaginative persons; extreme addiction to mathematical studies to those whose mental tendencies are just the reverse—men of dry and sapless minds;* but prescribed by Lord Bacon as a medicine

* Sir Wiliam Hamilton's Discussions. English edition, p. 258, &c.

for such as may be afflicted with "a wandering wit," or, as he elsewhere expresses it, are "bird-witted." The Bible, however, is a perennial fountain of health, and healing whatever may be the morbific tendencies of the mind. There can be no perfect system of education even for the mind, from which the Bible is excluded. This might be demonstrated, not only from the greatness of the ideas it evolves and discloses; from the purity, variety, vigour, and sublimity, of its style; but from the moral elevation of its distinctive and reigning spirit. There must be a proper adjustment—an interior harmony between the intellectual and moral forces, to develope the highest vigour of either; and a right state of the affections is indispensable, if not to perfect sanity of mind, to its utmost strength and keenest sagacity. The Rabbins say that the manna which fell in the wilderness, was divinely adapted to every man's taste. So the word of God—the bread of heaven, is divinely adapted to every man's intellectual habit. See what innumerable speculations in moral truth, of the utmost variety, beauty, sublimity, and value, filling numberless folios, in many tongues, have all been legitimately drawn from the sacred Scriptures; pure, fertilizing, life-giving streams, branching out from these inexhaustible fountains; as the river, which went out from Eden, was divided into four heads. Gen. ii. 10.

To see a man, who is not professionally bound to study the Scriptures, familiar with the several parts of the Bible; not only its doctrines and precepts, but its histories and prophecies, and the exact circumstances of their accomplishment—is a rare thing. For this there is no excuse whatever, in an educated Protestant community, where the people at large are not forbidden to study the Scriptures. There are many books—and even popular books, which we should blush to have read. But there is one book, which every man who can read should blush not to know familiarly, and in every part of its diversified revelations. That book is the Bible. The deep and diligent study of every portion of God's word—for it is all more precious than the gold of Ophir, and even the very dust of the stones of this temple of God glitters with heavenly radiance—would be followed by a visible and vast improvement, not only in purely spiritual knowledge, but of the natural powers. Every other study is comparatively contracted in its tendency and scope. This alone can impart to the various faculties, a complete and catholic education. Those who imbibe secular knowledge only, are like those who fed from the tables of the king of Babylon. There is nothing sacred in their aliment, and nothing striking in their aspect. But those who feed upon what some may choose to regard as the pulse and water of the word of God—will be found in the end, like the three children, "fairer and fatter in flesh than all the children which did eat the portion of the king's meat." Daniel i. 8—16.

We speak habitually of the moral and intellectual faculties; and the distinction is not only common but convenient. Still we should never lose sight of the fact that the soul is an indivisible unit, and that these various exercises are but different manifestations of the one indwelling spirit. It has often been remarked, that the Bible does not recognize that wide distinction between them, which obtains in our prevailing systems of philosophy, and in common parlance. Hence we frequently read of the thoughts of the heart and the desires of the mind; men are said to understand with the heart, and the heart is said to be enlightened with knowledge. On the other hand, they are spoken of as serving the Lord with all humility of mind, and receiving the word with all readiness of mind. Matt. xiii. 15; Rom. x. 10; 2 Cor. iv. 6; Acts xvii. 11; xx. 19. See Hodge on Romans, i. 21. So intimate indeed is the connection between the apprehensions of the mind, and the corresponding moral emotions—especially in regard to the most sublime and sacred truths—that it is often exceedingly difficult to draw the line between them. There is a wisdom, which may be called the wisdom of the heart. A tender heart and benevolent temper will sometimes not only surpass the wisdom of years, but anticipate the discoveries of ages. Thus, at the early age of fourteen, Edward the Sixth acknowledged principles of toleration, which Archbishop Cranmer, the counsellor of kings, could not understand, and which are far from being universally embraced, even at the present day. How did this English Josiah come to understand more than all his teachers? Simply, because his soul tutored his understanding, and this serene and comprehensive wisdom was the appropriate result.

The preceptive portions of the word of God requiring us to fulfil all righteousness, forbidding every transgression, and disobedience, are an argument of the goodness, scarcely less than of the holiness of God. Is it not a plain proof of goodness, that all his commands should be of such a nature, that obedience exalts us to glory, honour, and virtue; that he should enjoin nothing which it is not for our well-being to do; that he should forbid nothing which it is not for our well-being to forbear or to forego? And what is remarkable is that obedience should exalt us just in proportion as it is perfect and willing; and what is still more remarkable is that there should be nothing painful in it, provided it be voluntary, nothing servile or degrading in obedience, provided it be rendered to just authority. We can indeed conceive of no higher freedom than to have the soul subject to conscience, and conscience subject to God.

Serene will be our days and bright,
And happy will our nature be,
When love is an unerring light,
And joy its own security.

God himself—who is in the highest sense free and

the fountain of freedom to all his creatures—is yet obedient to the law of his own most excellent nature, in the exercise of that very freedom and in virtue of that very excellence. 1 Tim. ii. 13.

Examine the Bible, in any light and from any point of view, and it is infinitely remarkable as containing the earliest and only authentic history of our race; in the peerless majesty of its utterances concerning God; in its incomparable power over the human heart and conscience; in its unapproachable influence on the character of nations and races, and on the whole course of this world's history. Is it not remarkable that the Scriptures, written many of them in the infancy of our race, should not have been superseded by something later and better; that all the wit of man cannot go beyond them, as a scheme of salvation, or even as a book of moral duty and practical wisdom? Is it not still more remarkable that such a book should have emanated from such a people, from the Jews; and that nothing to compare with it should be found among the Greeks, or elsewhere; and that nothing to compare with it should be found among the uninspired books of the Jews themselves; that it should stand alone and aloft, in the firmament of letters, like the star which the wise men saw over the place where the Christ should be born? This is one of the many circumstances, which mark the Scriptures of the Old Testament, not less than the New, as unique and unparalleled in the intellectual history of mankind. It is only one of the manifold difficulties of infidelity—a thousand fold more insuperable than any of the difficulties of Scripture; and it is one which infidels never will be able to remove with all their art and industry, so long as history, sacred and profane, shall survive. It is only one of the many infallible proofs of the divine origin and authority of the Hebrew and Christian Scriptures. Is it not indeed a singular phenomenon? and is there not a wonderful assemblage of singular phenomena about the Christian system, both in its substance and history, as there was about the life and death of Christ himself, in whom the whole system centres, around whom it all revolves?

The Bible is demonstrably different from what it would have been; is, in many parts of its structure, in many of its doctrines, in much of its spirit, entirely the opposite of what it must have been, if it had been concocted by shrewd and sagacious men. Many of its details touching Jewish history and other things seem to us needless, especially when repeated with no remarkable or essential variation; while its notices on many other occasions, and on many other topics, which seem to us much more important and attractive, are extremely scanty, if any at all. What better evidence could we have that "the prophecy came not in old time by the will of man, but that holy men of God spake as they were moved by the Holy Ghost;" since we find just such difficulties in nature and providence; and

God himself has told us that his thoughts are not as our thoughts, nor his ways as our ways? 2 Pet. i. 21. Isa. lv. 8. When with this consideration we connect the remote and apparently antagonistic fact of the complete correspondence and harmony running through the Bible histories, such as no human foresight or forethought could have contrived; the miracle of the gift of tongues, for example, prefiguring the ingrafting of the Gentiles, as the miraculous confusion of tongues had prefigured their excision, the proof of the superhuman character of these records becomes altogether irresistible. Acts ii. 1–13. Gen xi. 1–9.

It is not uncommon for modern infidels to speak of the Christian religion as obsolete; not coincident with their scientific conclusions, and not equal to their schemes of philanthropy. As an illustration, we may refer to one of the latest and most arrogant forms of atheistic unbelief, that known as the Positive Philosophy of Auguste Comte, which affirms that mankind in their normal development pass through three successive stages, 1st. the Theological; 2d. the Metaphysical; 3d. the Scientific. When therefore they become Scientific, they must of necessity cease to be Christian. To all this we may reply:—

In the first place, that the Bible does not purport to be a revelation of scientific, but of spiritual truth; that the glorious gospel of the blessed God is the gospel of our salvation; that science belongs properly to the domain of reason; that a religious revelation is addressed primarily to the moral sense, and has to do with moral truth and with moral duty.

In the second place, that it is not a little remarkable that no scientific error ever should have been positively fastened upon it, alluding as it does to every department of nature animate and inanimate; rehearsing the creation of the world; repeatedly recounting the wonders of the universe; and touching, in prophecy or history, or both, on every important dynasty and nation which has ever existed.

In the third place, that those who have expended all their eloquence, learning, and wit, in the endeavour to discredit and destroy it, as Volney and Gibbon, have done it involuntary service; rendered unconscious tribute to its truth, and accumulated unwilling testimony to its divinity; that Christianity is true, and therefore immortal; that it has been assailed in turn by Judaism and Paganism; by Herod and by Julian; by secret stratagem and by open force; from within and from without; by persecution, heresy, and schism; by the treachery of false brethren and by the violence of professed enemies; and that it yet survives, not in decrepitude and decline, but in unwasting vigour and invincible might; that let a man of science, like Kepler, or Laplace, or Lavoisier, simply pursue his scientific investigations, question nature in Bacon's noble phrase, without once thinking of the Bible, and it will be amazing to remark the strict correspondence between his most mature conclusions and the Bible testimonies in regard to the same subjects. The recent testimony of our distinguished countryman, Lieutenant Maury, on this point, is of the highest value; coinciding, as it does with the recorded sentiments of Sir Humphrey Davy, Sir Isaac Newton, and Lord Bacon; not one of whom was the less religious because scientific. Bacon's works generally, in all of which not a sentence or sentiment will be found in disparagement of the Christian religion, and especially his essay on Atheism, should be deeply pondered by every educated young man, who may be in danger from the significant silence of Humboldt, or the recorded blasphemies of Comte. "The Sciences," says Cousin, "so far from turning us away from religion, conduct us to it. Physics with their laws, mathematics with their sublime ideas, especially philosophy which cannot take a single step without encountering universal and necessary principles, are so many stages on the way to Deity, and thus to speak, so many temples, in which homage is perpetually paid to Him." *

In the fourth place, that in experience, the Bible is found to carry with it all other blessings, whether to an individual or to a community; for this world, as well as the world to come; that while it primarily contemplates the soul and the spiritual inter-

* Lectures on the True, Beautiful, and Good, p. 99.

ests of men; the forgiveness of sin; peace of conscience; hope toward God; support in trouble, in sickness, and in death; together with an inheritance beyond the grave, incorruptible, undefiled, and that fadeth not away; it incidentally, but invariably and inevitably, carries other blessings in its train. To an individual, it not only brings peace of conscience —a never-failing spring of the sweetest enjoyment— but ordinarily the public respect and confidence; and that too, just in proportion, as the real nature of this religion is understood, and to the purity and fulness, with which the individual is believed to have embraced it. To a community, it brings all public and social blessings. In the exact proportion in which it prevails, industry, honesty, thrift, chastity, temperance, mutual good-will, intellectual improvement, equal laws, social elevation, civil and religious liberty prevail. 1 Tim. iv. 10. Its influence in improving the condition of society; preserving peace among the nations; softening national prejudices; affirming the unity of the race, and teaching the brotherhood of the nations; giving rise to wholesome laws, and disposing men to desire and observe them; promoting benevolent institutions, for the relief of the wretched and the helpless—almshouses, hospitals, asylums for the blind, the deaf, the dumb, and the insane; the consecration of philosophical discoveries and scientific inventions to merciful uses; all these are to be taken into the account. Mankind have been much more happy since the advent of our Saviour, and Christian nations have been incomparably more happy and more elevated in mind and morals, than other nations. Unfaithful, as many nominal Christians are, real Christians are still, as they have ever been, as they must ever be, the salt of the earth and the light of the world. For the soul of the true believer is a divine palimpsest, from which the base characters of sin have been at least partially erased, to make room for the beautiful inscriptions of holiness.

In the fifth place, the fundamental lessons of Nature, as well as of Scripture, presuppose and demand no acquaintance whatever with the abstruser parts of science. Nature and Scripture were both designed for the instruction and delight, not of a select circle, but of all mankind; and the wisdom of the common Author of both is conspicuous in this common characteristic. The peasant, not less than the philosopher, can admire the wisdom of God in the grand though familiar forms and arrangements of nature; in the wonderful instinct of bees and birds and beasts. In early days, not less than now, in primitive and simple, not less than in later and scientific times, the undimmed glories of majestic nature, of night, of the ocean, and of the mountain, the sounding cataract and the sunny slope, spoke in audible accents and intelligible voice, to the heart of man. David, Isaiah, and Homer felt as deeply the magnificence and the beauty of these objects as Milton, Chalmers or Brewster. So the prime and obvious revelations of the word of God; the great truths of Catholic Christianity, which stand out from the general level of inspired Scripture, as the stars and the mountains from the landscape of nature; in their simple grandeur, may strike the mind of the pious cottager, with as deep a sense of awe and as delicious a sense of beauty, as that with which they fill the admiring soul of the learned philosopher or Rabbi. The just, the final and the only conclusion is, that there is no real conflict between Scripture and Science—the word and the works of God—and that any apparent discrepancy arises from our misconception of the true teachings of one or of both.

LECTURE II.

DIVINE REVELATION SPECIALLY SUITED TO THE NATURE AND NEEDS OF THE SOUL.

FROM this general and distant view of the subject, let us pass on to the consideration of particular truths. This is indeed like fixing the eye distinctly, for a while, on "one bright particular star," after it has been wearied by gazing on the general glories of the midnight sky.

By way of simple and easy illustration, let us take the first doctrine of all religion, natural and revealed—the being of a God—more precisely the Bible idea of God, in all his infinite perfections as revealed to Moses :—

"The Lord, the Lord God, merciful and gracious, long-suffering and slow to anger, abundant in goodness and truth, keeping mercy for thousands, forgiving iniquity and transgression and sin and that will by no means clear the guilty." Ex. xxxiv. 6, 7.

Now just conceive of a man cut off from all knowledge or hearing of God altogether ; into whose mind the sublime conception of God had never entered, suddenly having a full revelation of this all-glorious Being and of all his adorable perfections. It would be like the wide shining of the mid-day sun, rising on the noon of night; at once bursting forth in his meridian splendour from the deep bosom of all-surrounding darkness.

In the second book of his very remarkable treatise "Concerning the Nature of the Gods," Cicero has preserved to us a singularly interesting extract from a lost work of Aristotle. "If there were beings, who had always lived underground, in convenient, nay magnificent dwellings, adorned with statues and pictures, and every thing that belongs to prosperous life, but who had never come above ground; who had heard however, by fame and report, of the being and power of the gods; if at a certain time the portals of the earth being thrown open, they had been able to emerge from those hidden abodes to the regions inhabited by us; when suddenly they had seen the earth, the seas, and the sky; had perceived the vastness of the clouds and the force of the winds; had contemplated the sun, his magnitude and beauty, and still more his effectual power, that it is he who makes the day by the diffusion of his light through the whole sky; and when night had darkened the earth, should then behold the whole heavens, studded and adorned with stars, and the various lights of the waxing and waning moon, the rising and the setting of all these heavenly bodies; and their courses fixed and immutable in all eternity;

when, I say, they should see these things, truly they would believe that there are gods, and that these so great things are their works.* Not only does it illuminate and exalt, but it mightily fortifies and draws the mind to conceive of God, not a mere presence like the air, not a mere general name for the unknown forces of nature; but a perfect and personal being, in conscious existence before the mountains were brought forth, and destined to exist after the dissolution of the universe; full of majesty and grace, glorious in holiness, fearful in praises, doing wonders, and yet not far from any one of us; in whom we live and move and have our being, our Father in Heaven!

This grand conception, this fundamental truth, this primary fact is not formally propounded in divine revelation, but everywhere assumed and proceeded upon. Gen. i. 1. And so the wonders rise as we ascend, step by step, the mystic ladder of inspired Scripture, Gen. xxviii. 12, one end resting on the earth, the other reaching to the skies; as we scrutinize the several doctrines of this matchless volume in their isolated grandeur or in their combined and reflected glory. One God the Father of all, infinite, eternal, and unchangeable; the Father of lights; the Father of mercies; the God of glory;

* The translation is by our American Cicero, Edward Everett. Appropriate reference is made to this passage of Aristotle in a beautiful essay of Addison. Spectator. No. 465.

One Lord Jesus Christ; the Only Begotten of the Father; full of grace and truth; his co-equal and co-eternal Son; in the ineffable majesty of his person; in the unspotted beauty of his life; in the greatness, the multitude, and gracious character of his miracles; in the divine Majesty, the unfathomable depth, and the inexhaustible power of his spoken words; words which are this day spirit and life, to us as truly and as largely as to them that heard him; in his life of holy obedience and in his death of gracious expiation, equally marvellous and alike unparalleled. One blessed and eternal Spirit, proceeding from the Father and the Son; who, with life-giving energy, moved upon the face of the waters; who garnished the heavens and formed the crooked serpent; the Source of all created light and life and love; in the unsearchable wisdom and greatness of his operations; in his power to make alive the soul dead in trespasses and sins, to subdue its iniquities, to expel its corruptions, and to create it anew in the glorious image of God. This one God, in three persons, the same in substance, equal in power and glory, Creator, Redeemer, and Sanctifier, revealed as the proper and only object of religious worship; as the proper and all-sufficient portion of the creature, his heritage and joy for ever; the incarnation, the atonement, and the intercession of the Lord Jesus Christ; his power and glory as Mediator; the gracious office of the Holy Ghost, as

Sanctifier, Comforter, and Guide, his cleansing efficacy, his vital ray, his healing unction.

Not less wonderful is this revelation in what it discloses concerning the origin, history, and destiny of man, than in what it makes known in regard to the being, the nature, the will, and the works of God; in the doctrine which it delivers, of an immortal, undivided, complete existence of man in body and soul after death; in a body raised and renovated, but still ours and recognized as ours; in a soul not as now contracted and impure, but expanded and immaculate, still ours, and rejoiced in as truly and consciously our own; in its recognition of our poor fallen human nature, just as it is in all its degradation, helplessness, and woe; in its taking up the puzzling problem of man's estate of sin and misery, and furnishing a satisfying solution and the only solution of it; in its revelation of a remedy for all our diseases and a balm for all our wounds!

The wonders which God exhibits to our contemplation in the world of nature, would seem more amazing, were our perceptive faculties enlarged and sharpened. In certain cases, the chief inconveniences, arising from the imperfection of our bodily organs, have been at least partially remedied by mechanical instruments.

The microscope and the telescope have in turn revealed to us treasures of heavenly wisdom, invisible to the naked eye; of a wisdom which is alike able to crowd with wonders a single drop of water, and the boundless expanse of the starry skies. So in regard to the infinite realities, revealed to our faith in the Scriptures. They can never be comprehended. They can never be numbered. They can never be measured. But they are not therefore to be overlooked; only to be all the more diligently pondered, and all the more highly prized.

It may be that the more thoughtful of us, in early youth, dreaded lest increase of years and of wisdom should dispel the majesty, which invested the objects of revelation to our immature minds. This feeling is not only natural to a thoughtful mind, imbued with the gentle sympathies, and the tender sentiments of natural piety, awake to the magnificence of the outer world, of sky, and plain, and river, bathed in the splendours of the rising or the setting sun; and alive to the still purer glories, the more tender light, the more perfect loveliness that beams upon us, from the face of heavenly truth—inspired Scripture—but true in regard to every other religion known to history except that revealed in the Bible. No other can be consistently maintained, or adhered to in consistency with the progress of scientific intelligence. We know that the religious systems of India at the present day are so vitally bound together with demonstrable errors in various departments of natural science, that the only alternative with an educated native is infidelity or Christianity. Nor is this by any means a new or a rare phenomenon. Neander tells us that "the popular religions of antiquity answered only for a certain stage of culture. When the nations in the course of their progress had passed beyond this, the necessary consequence was a dissevering of the spirit from the religious traditions. In the case of the more quiet and equable development of the Oriental mind, so tenacious of the old, the opposition between the mythic religion of the people, and the secret theosophic doctrines of a priestly caste who gave direction to the popular conscience, might exist for centuries without change. But among the more excitable nations of the West, intellectual culture, so soon as it attained to a certain degree of independence, must fall into collision with the mythic religion handed down from the infancy of the people.

In our callow youth we have perhaps wondered how the revelations of Scripture, so glorious and so dear to us, appeared to grown men, and feared lest

> " Years that bring the philosophic mind,"

might enable us to overmaster them, to see through them, to rise above them; and there has been something of surprise mingled with our delight to find that the only effect of the exercise of our improved faculties on these sublime subjects, has been kindred to the revelations of the microscope and the telescope in regard to the miracles of nature. Together with the enlargement of our spiritual vision, has there been a corresponding increase in the apparent magnitude of spiritual objects. The oldest and the most intelligent Christian, Sir Isaac Newton or Chalmers or Edwards, is as far from a complete mastery of the grand truths which relate to the being, the perfections, and the works of God, in the two distinct departments of nature and grace, as a little child.

In their infinite elevation, in their unfathomable significance, in their manifold relations, and in their abiding results, the truths of divine revelation transcend not only the human understanding but the ken of an angel. 1 Pet. i. 12; Eph. iii. 10, 19; Rev. iv. 8–11. As our impressions of the pomp and prodigality of nature, everywhere teeming with life and with prolific powers, are heightened by the revelations of the microscope and by the illuminated page of the firmament, written over within and without in the glorious handwriting of God; so the more improved our spiritual faculties, the more extended our spiritual knowledge, the more august will be our conceptions, the more exalted our impressions of revealed truth. The stronger and the more exercised our spiritual faculties, the more marvellous and splendid our spiritual discoveries. But the last and highest discovery of all, will be that this is verily a love that passeth knowledge, that ours is verily a God that hideth himself though it be in a pavilion of light, that we cannot find out the Almighty to perfection, and we shall finally exclaim with Paul, when we have reached the highest point in our future advancement, "Oh! the depth of the riches both of the wisdom and knowledge of God! how unsearchable are his judgments and his ways past finding out!" Rom. xi. 33.

The conscious wretchedness of man in his fallen state is a truth attested by all the feelings of the heart, expressed under all the forms of speech, acknowledged by every system of philosophy, assumed in every scheme of religion; lamented in the poetry, recorded in the history of every nation; the universal sentiment because the universal experience of the race. The noblest work of God even in his ruin, man still bears the mark of his primitive and princely glory. His physical organization, his intellectual faculties, his social affections, his moral powers, his indestructible sense of religion, found wherever he is found, evinced amidst ignorance and vice, blindness, and barbarism, prompt him always and everywhere to seek after God. Bound to the earth by fetters of corruption, but still lifting an eye of devotion and hope to heaven, the victim of sin and the born thrall of Satan, he still in conscience recognizes the just authority of God. And though the currents of this his nature are now all turned awry, its sweet harmonies disturbed and jarred, its integrity lost, its powers enfeebled, its heavenly peace fled, its once unspotted purity defiled, yet does the soul of man, by its conscious craving and continual cry, show that he was meant to be the minister, that it was meant to be the temple of God. The mind of man has many mansions, imagination, taste, sentiment, a capacity of perceiving and enjoying various species of truths poetical, mathematical, moral, and divine. This we feel when we gaze on "the universal book of knowledge fair," the face of nature, the bright sky, and the fruitful earth. But these mansions of the mind are either tenantless of the noblest truths which should dwell in them, or they are occupied by hideous monsters, depraved affections, and loathsome errors.

The affinity of the soul for universal truth, environed as it is by mysteries in every object and by ignorance in every science, and most of all in theology, the vast disproportion between its present powers and desires, its aspirations and attainments, are an unfailing source of inward fretting and disquiet, of resentful humiliation not of sweet humility, of secret corroding bitterness, of an ulcerous and ungovernable discontent. There is now a schism in the soul itself which man can neither disguise nor heal, deep discord among its faculties and forces; a dissatisfaction which he would allay, a disorder which he would remove but cannot!

Now there is a striking congruity between the human soul, with its vast capacities of knowledge and enjoyment; with its incessant yearnings after what is great, what is true, and what is good, and the Christian religion, in its revelation of infinite greatness, of absolute truth, and of the supreme good—an admirable correspondence, as of the echo to the sound; a visible adaptation, as of the respiratory organs to the vital air; as of the form of the key to the wards of the lock; as the soil to the seed; the ear to music, the eye to beauty, and the heart to love. The revelation of God, with all its truths and sanctions, consolations and gifts, is addressed to the soul of man. The soul of man, with all its instincts, capacities, desires, and needs, responds to the revelation of God.

It requires no elaborate analysis of the faculties of the soul to evince this spiritual correspondence—no partial appeal to select circles—to limited classes—to individuals highly cultivated and rarely endowed. All that we have to do, is simply to go forth and make known the gospel call to the religious consciousness of mankind at large; to address the common reason—the general conscience burdened, polluted, enthralled, trembling; to speak to the throbbing heart of the mixed multitude; to knock at the door of ordinary, lowly, human affection. Then present the grand scheme brought to light in the Gospel—Christ the power of God and the wisdom of God to every one that believeth. Only sound out the superhuman revelations of THE BOOK—that system of Scriptural doctrine of which Christ and he crucified is the Alpha and Omega. Only go to man, high or low, savage or civilized, let the powers, the passions, and the aspirations of this, our common human nature, be deeply stirred; let them heave like the billowy sea—the quaking earth—the volcanic mountain. Then bring the grand

and soothing, the awful and gracious truths of Christ before the mind—softer than the melody of the whispering wind, as it creeps from flower to flower; more beautiful than the light that dwells in the day-star, will be the voice of God, uttered in the word—will be the grace of God, echoed in the heart.

A keen sense of literary beauty, even in the Bible, is not piety. A man may enjoy the Bible, or the eloquent exposition of the Bible, with the greatest zest, and yet not have a single spark of love to God or faith in Christ. There is in the Bible, a moral force entirely independent of rhetorical beauty—a penetrating power—a voice of command, which springs from its divinity, and seals it and proves it. The exceeding preciousness of the Bible, to the poor and miserable, the down-cast and the down-trodden, can hardly be understood or conceived of, by the prosperous and the gay, the worldly minded and the proud hearted. What could Dives, clothed in purple and faring sumptuously every day, know of the soul of Lazarus, feeding on the heavenly promises, while in want of what is needful for the body; and soon to be borne by angels from the rich man's gate to Abraham's bosom? We naturally cling to the earth, and it requires for the most part, a forcible blow to detach us from it. The sons and daughters of affliction need the sunlight, that beams from the loving face of the Man of Sorrows, the Friend and Saviour of sinners. They need his sweet sympathy. Disappointed and unhappy here, they look to heaven. Forsaken of man, they take refuge in God. Weary and heavy laden, they turn to him, who gives rest to the soul. Such are truly blessed; led by trouble to rest; by want of friends, to "an innumerable company" of saints and angels; by human desertion, to the companionship of the Lord of glory; by poverty on earth, to durable riches in heaven; by shame, and sorrow, and death, to honour, and joy, and life everlasting.

The trifling, the self satisfied, the shallow minded, the grossly sensual, the deeply deluded, may heed not, may feel not, this spiritual accordance of the revelations of God and the needs of the soul; for they have not the depth of conviction on any subject; the seriousness, the heart knowledge, to hearken to the word of God in the Bible, or to listen to the voice of God uttering his oracles from the Shekinah of conscience. In the great events of life, when the strongest passions, such as fear, remorse, and grief, are stirred to their depths, nothing but the Christian religion can soothe and still the soul. Books of amusement and gay exhibitions may serve to occupy the vacant mind, and business of importance may employ more serious hours. But there are seasons, when both of these are felt to be unsatisfying and impertinent; when grander aims and graver cares than belong to this fleeting scene, are felt and owned to be the proper portion of the immortal spirit.

The largest rivers empty into the sea; so the deepest feelings terminate in religion, or tend toward it. In the wonder working providence of God, men are often led to lasting happiness by transient troubles—the loss of property, friends, or children; and this is the use which the wise will always strive to make of the adverse dispensations of heaven; adopting the prayer of Moses: "So teach us to number our days that we may apply our hearts unto wisdom." Deep as is the heart of man, the Christian religion is still deeper. It may have little attraction for the gay, the superficial, the light minded; but the old, the disappointed, the wretched, the sadly and the truly wise—who have tested and sounded human life, and have been taught by bitter experience to sigh for a better portion—taught by heavenly grace, turn with irrepressible eagerness to the consolatory and sublime hope of immortality.

There is not a promise of the word of God, which has not inspired the heart of many an afflicted saint with unspeakable comfort. How often has a single text of Scripture, made the object of an appropriating faith, darted an instant sunshine into the darkened heart! As hunger naturally disposes us to seek food, as thirst to crave drink, as weariness to long for rest; so a wise sorrow, a sadness of the heart, sanctified and blessed, prepares us to desire the bread of heaven, causes us to cry for that living water of which if a man drink he shall never thirst. There is a constant intercourse by faith and prayer, between heaven and earth; as the rain comes down from heaven and returns again in vapour; so grace comes down into the heart and returns in the fragrant breath of prayer and praise.

No one need ever fear that he will exhaust the Christian religion; that he will get to the bottom of it, that he will find it old and impotent, effete and barren. It is a perpetual novelty, not indeed in the substance of its revelations, but in our personal apprehension and experience of them. On every occasion of life, which shakes and startles us, and discovers, as by a flash of lightning, the mysteries of our moral being, and exhibits to our own eyes the unsuspected depths of our own nature, shows us our mortal weakness and our immortal strength, then will the authentic revelation of Him, who was the Son of God, and the Man of Sorrows, of him who at one moment wept by the grave of Lazarus, and the next moment said unto him, "Lazarus, come forth!" then will this revelation appear to us in a light new and fresh and wonderful, in aspect beautiful and benign, sublime in its dimensions, expanding on every side beyond the most enlarged capacities of the soul, an inscrutable, an eternal, an infinite reality; recognized by the clear spirit, as true when most it needs, discerns, and delights in the truth.

The grandeur of the Christian revelation may be inferred from the fact, not only that it has seemed grandest to the purest and most exalted of our race, but that it seems grandest even to them, when the mind is in its purest and loftiest mood, when it rises above its ordinary level—when, conscious of its own inherent, spiritual dignity, it looks up in filial worship to the Father of Spirits, whose eternal Son hath taken to himself our nature. In the material universe, we see the glory of God considered absolutely—his eternal power and Godhead. In scripture, we see his glory as it is in the face of Jesus Christ. His grace as a Saviour sheds a sweet and tender light over every other attribute. This is indeed "the mystery of godliness—God manifest in the flesh; justified in the spirit; seen of angels; preached unto the Gentiles; believed on in the world; received up into glory. 1 Tim. iii. 16.

The Christian religion is myriad-sided. It may be considered as an instrument of present and palpable good; as the cement and conservator of human society. It touches and connects the most distant extremes. It at once teaches man true humility, by revealing the true God in his true glory; and it lifts him to an inward and abiding elevation, by conscious communion with the God whom he adores, like the rainbow that spans the sky and seems to touch the earth, at once connecting and beautifying both. The Christian religion, in the highest sense and in its purest exercise, is the believing worship of God, revealed in Christ as reconciling the world unto himself, not imputing their trespasses unto them. It is therefore the highest attainment of a redeemed creature; the supreme blessedness of the adopted sons of God. The love of God, shed abroad in the heart by the Holy Ghost, is not only the most sublime but the most delightful affection of which the human soul is capable. It is that water of life of which if a man drink he shall never thirst. It is that wine, of which the miraculous wine of Cana may be taken as the symbol and the pledge, of all the gifts of God, the flower and the crown.

There is hardly any experience of human life, there is hardly any form of human sorrow, which does not impart additional significance and sweetness to the Christian Scriptures. Many a man has read the narratives of our Lord's miraculous cures, with comparative indifference when in health; and when worn by sickness, he has learned to peruse the same passages with the deepest sympathy and delight. But whatever our outward lot, no one can truly understand the Scriptures without the internal unction of the Holy Ghost; no one can rightly enter into the truths they contain without His spiritual illumination and guidance. We cannot, for instance, receive the doctrine of total depravity, without such an apprehension of the evil of our own hearts as no man can attain without the teaching of the Holy Ghost; and he who has been the subject of that gracious enlightening, feels that nothing that the Scriptures affirm of the depravity of the heart is too strong, because he knows something of the evil of his own heart. Nor will any man ever learn to estimate aright the preciousness of Christ, who has not been taught of God, to hate the pollution of sin, and strive after inward, absolute, universal holiness.

The word of God is a well-ordered armoury, in which we may find a weapon fitted and furbished, for every occasion. 1 Tim. iii. 17. Eph. v. 11–17. In having the Scriptures, we are richer than we know. There may be truths in the Scriptures, which we have not yet learned to understand, to feel, to prize, simply because we have not yet been placed in circumstances to make us need their power and taste their sweetness. In passing over the field of the word of God, and little heeding the precious treasures imbedded in its hidden depths, we are like the simple Aborigines of our own broad land who roamed, careless and thoughtless, over mines of golden ore.

The Bible is a firmament, in which new stars of surpassing brilliancy are continually coming forth to our view; and it may be that the light that dwells in some—the unfulfilled prophecies—has not travelled to the earth, to the present time. Doubtless our understanding of the manifold wisdom of God, revealed in his word, will be advancing through all eternity, in due proportion to the expansion of our faculties, and our personal experience of an exceeding and eternal weight of glory. No other language than that of God himself can adequately set forth the present experience of a child of God; his sense of the sinfulness of sin, of what he owes to the sovereign grace of God the Father; of what Christ, his Saviour, is made unto him of God; his habitual impression of the incomparable glories of his Saviour's person, and the exceeding greatness of the reward that there is even now in keeping his commandments.

"Beloved, now are we the sons of God, and it doth not yet appear what we shall be, but we know that when he shall appear, we shall be like him, for we shall see him as he is." 1 John iii. 2.

LECTURE III.

TRANSCENDENT NATURE OF THE DOCTRINES OF DIVINE REVELATION.

THE transcendent nature of the Christian doctrines, so far from being an objection, constitutes a peculiar and a necessary proof of the divine origin of the Christian revelation. The sphere of thought of a man of genius is altogether inconceivable to an ordinary mind; how much more the divine counsels to the most exalted created intelligence! There are accordingly things in the Bible, which previous to experience we should not expect to find there; and other things are not there which we should naturally anticipate. This singular character of the sacred record is conditioned in the first place on the perfection of God, its Author; in the second, on the ignorance, weakness, and guilt of man, to whom it is addressed. It is a supernatural revelation of the infinite and all-perfect God, to fallen and finite man. This we should remember when reading it, and therefore not be suprised at the presence of mysteries.

The Apostle Paul repeatedly affirms that the revelations of God are beyond the reach of human philosophy; that the wit of man is wholly incompetent, not merely to discover, but to understand them; that they can neither be anticipated nor received by the wisdom of men, and that we cannot possibly attain to the saving knowledge of them but by the unction of the Holy One. This is unquestionably true in regard to many of the facts and doctrines which the Bible discloses. They are such as men never would have suspected; such as they never could have dared to look for in a revelation from God; such as in fact they could not possibly have affirmed beforehand to be there without the utmost impiety. And this, not because there is any fact or doctrine delivered in the Bible, unworthy of the holiness or the majesty of God, but chiefly because of the transcendent grace, the unsearchable wisdom, the ineffable condescension, the far-reaching providence of God, seemingly and for a season perplexed, tortuous, standing still, like the pillar of cloud, but ever keeping the purposed end in view, spreading over nations, comprehending centuries; slowly unrolled and unravelled, but never for a moment suspended or slumbering, never lost sight of, never defeated; working out its secret and its declared purposes, alike by enemies and friends; at times swiftly and conspicuously; at times obscurely and slowly; suffering long ages to intervene, and seeming slack concerning his promises; then riding upon the wings of the wind, making the clouds his chariots, and causing a nation to be born in a day. What mortal could have anticipated the first, the central truth of revealed religion, that of God manifest in the flesh dying for our sins? Or having conceived of such an event, would have dared to utter it in words? Who would not have feared that the lightnings of heaven, the hot thunderbolts of God, would instantly blast him for giving utterance to such an amazing imagination? How hard do we find it now ourselves fully to believe this capital article of our creed, with all its awful and consoling consequences, and to make our fellow men believe it, when it is not an unauthorized imagination of the thought of the heart, but a recognized doctrine of the Christian church; when it is not cloudily unfolded or scantily witnessed or feebly affirmed, but shone upon by a perfect flood of day, the grand lesson, the governing idea, the paramount truth of all the Evangelists and of all the Apostles alike!

In the very difficulties of belief we find our answer to the infidel and sceptic, in the very fact that the most characteristic and the most obtrusive and unquestionable doctrines of the Bible are so hard to be understood, are so apt to be wrested, are so often and so obstinately and so bitterly rejected; on this very ground do we build our argument, for the divine origin and the binding authority of this revelation. For God's thoughts are not as our thoughts, nor his ways as our ways. If mere men—uninspired men had made this book, it would have been more like their work. It would have been more in harmony with their preconceptions. It would have been more congenial to their tastes. But being the work of God, it is like God, in knowledge, wisdom, holiness, goodness, and truth. It has the stamp and seal of his supreme divinity on every page; it has his sacred superscription, his uncreated image on every doctrine.

From their heavenly import and origin, from their superhuman nature, they never could be divined by the wit of man. Even a wise man's counsels are beyond the ken of an idiot; a liberal man's spirit, above the comprehension of a churl. How far above, out of sight, are the eternal counsels of the most high God! the wisdom and grace of the "Father of lights, from whom cometh down every good and every perfect gift."

That which constitutes the proper and peculiar glory of the gospel, is its revelation of a class of truths, of all others the most needful, precious, and high, which the most enlightened and thoughtful of the children of men never could find out; which were inaccessible to the human understanding in their very nature, wholly unattainable otherwise than by the gift, incommunicable save by the wisdom and the grace, of God. The characters graven on the gospel are incomparably more glorious than those impressed on the material universe. For if the eternal power and Godhead of Jehovah are clearly seen in sun, moon and stars, the flowers and birds and trees and sparkling waters, his tender mercy beams brightest in the gospel of his Son: and if the law, which as a glorious mirror at once revealed and reflected his unspotted holiness, was given by Moses, grace and truth came by Jesus Christ.

The very design of a supernatural revelation from God is to disclose truths beyond the unaided ken of man; to unveil what otherwise would remain for ever secret. And just in proportion to the sacredness, the vitality, the elevation, and the transcendent preciousness of the truths revealed, is their seeming remoteness from the ordinary apprehensions of the human mind. The body of revealed truths which specifically constitute the gospel of our salvation, which refer more directly to the constitution of the person of Christ, God and man in two natures yet one person for ever; and which turn upon the nature and design of the work of Christ, dying for our sins according to the Scriptures, and rising again from the dead a divine Victor over death and over *him* that had the power of death, even the Devil, the present lapsed state of human nature through the original offence of one man, whose sin in eating the forbidden fruit "brought death into the world and all our woe;" the indispensable need of the Holy Ghost to cleanse and sanctify our infected nature; the whole nature of our ingrafting into Christ by faith; our effectual calling, adoption, justification, sanctification, peace of conscience, and assured hope of a blessed immortality—these things pertain to the gospel properly and peculiarly. They are absolutely its own, without the obscurest hint in any of the eloquent voices of the material world, without trace or footprint in any path that uninstructed man had trodden.

From the necessity of the case therefore, unless we get our information from the Bible, we must remain in utter ignorance on subjects of everlasting moment to us all. The distinctive doctrines of divine revelation, are of such a transcendent character—so remote from the apprehension of any created mind—so entirely without the faintest hint or notice in all nature, that they never can be known at all if they are not known from inspired Scripture. The constitution of the divine nature—the doctrine of the Holy Trinity, of three persons and one essence, the same in substance, equal in power and glory, which underlies and interpenetrates the whole scheme of redemption by Christ Jesus—is a doctrine of which there is no trace in nature, no shadow in reason, and no prophecy in man.

There is another view of this subject incomparably more awful and appalling. The difficulty in the way of our anticipating the gracious counsels of heaven which we have just glanced at, is one which arises mainly from their superhuman elevation, from their unfathomable riches in glory. But the difficulty which I wish now to point out, is one which inheres not in the subject but in us, having its foundation in our depravity, and foolishness, and slowness of heart to believe all that the prophets of God have taught. The invisible God has afforded us in the creatures with their endless diversities of form, colour, habit, instinct, and element, with their varied classes, ranks, natures, and degrees of intelligence, a clear and beautiful mirror of his wisdom, so that such as possessed a single spark of sound judgment, might be hurried away into the involuntary adoration of himself. Rom. i. 20; 1 Cor. i. 21. But how far this is from the truth, let the sad experience of all heathen nations bear witness. The wisest of them have been able to rise little if at all above the most illiterate and debased, in their apprehensions of the true nature and right worship of God. Egypt, the cradle of knowledge and the arts, worshipped the most despised animals, the most loathsome reptiles; and the great nations of classic antiquity feigned innumerable gods, like unto themselves, vain, licentious, and bloody-minded. The sense of man, which is so strong and sagacious in regard to earthly things, is inexpressibly weak and dark in its apprehensions of things heavenly. "The sense of man," in a passage quoted by Lord Bacon, "is aptly said to resemble the sun, which openeth and revealeth the terrestrial globe, but obscureth and concealeth the celestial; so doth the sense discover natural things, but darken and shut up divine."

It appears, therefore, that men, even the wisest and the most cultivated of them, not less than the multitude, are apt not merely to overlook or mistake, but to corrupt and reject the truth; and this, not merely in regard to the obscurer and lower lessons graven on the creation, but equally in regard to the clearer and higher revelations of the gospel. For this very reason does the apostle call the proclamation of the glorious gospel of the blessed God—that which alone reveals his well-beloved Son as the Author and Finisher of faith—the preaching of foolishness. It does indeed seem foolishness to the wise men of this world, who scruple not to tax with folly the sacred truth of God, drunk with false confidence, and blind with ignorant rage. What distinctive doctrine of the gospel is there—what doctrine so plainly revealed, so precious to his saints, so essential to his truth and glory, that men held in reputation for wisdom and honour have not rejected—openly, obstinately, blasphemously rejected? What can seem more absurd to human reason than that God should take to himself our nature, and as a man should die; that the life of the world should be obnoxious to death; that the very light of heaven should be extinguished in preternatural darkness; that the righteousness of God should be covered over with the likeness of sin; that the chastisement of our peace should be inflicted on the Holy One; that the Bringer of salvation, the Giver of the blessing, should be made sin, and subject to the curse for us; and that in this way, and this only, men are to be redeemed from death and made partakers of a happy immortality; sin is to be destroyed, and righteousness to reign, and death, and the curse, to be swallowed up for ever! Nevertheless, the God-enlightened, the God-anointed know, that the gospel is the supreme wisdom of God, though that wisdom be veiled in mystery from the vision of the wise—a wisdom whose holy heights scan, nay rise above the heavens themselves, and into whose fathomless depths, the angels desire to look. Of all mysteries in religion, this is the sum and the chief, that, "when we were without strength, in due time Christ died for the ungodly."

The revelations of God are beyond the reach of human philosophy, and contravene the conclusions of human reason, not only in their greatness and majesty, but in the method and measure of their manifestation. This may be illustrated in what may be styled Evangelic obscurities.

There are many practical difficulties of this sort which strike the minds not only of open infidels, who studiously hunt for objections, but of plain people and even devout Christians, who would gladly know, believe, and do the truth. There is a class of men who have never felt the deep significance of human life; who have never conscientiously striven to know their duty toward God and to do it; who read the Bible and hear the gospel, not to learn the truth but merely to cavil, to trifle, to show their ingenuity, to gratify their vanity, to scatter fire-brands, arrows, and death; and say, Am not I in sport? Now I have not a word for such as these, except to say, "Behold ye despisers, and wonder, and perish!" "fools make a mock at sin and God will bring every secret thing into judgment." But there is another class to whom we cannot refuse the tribute of our respect and sympathy. It is those who honestly meditate on the word and providence of God, and are at once perplexed and pained by the difficulties which they find in both. That God should have reserved the full revelation of the gospel for four thousand years is a providential fact of marked character, and is in direct conflict with every natural anticipation. It has accordingly "given pause" to many a thoughtful mind. In the long lapse of time from the apostasy and the promise, to the incarnation and sacrifice of the Redeemer, many have found matter of sad and troubled thought. Now it is not so much my concern, to vindicate this dispensation, to assign the probable grounds and reasons of it, to show that the lesson to be taught us of the imbecility of the human understanding in relation to divine things, of the impotence of man to devise a way of salvation, and to order his life according to the rule of righteousness, was of sufficient moment to explain and to justify it; or that such a preparation would naturally dispose and fit the world to receive the revealed Redeemer with becoming sensibility and gladness—all of which is unquestionably true and of the highest importance; nor to insist upon the retro-active virtue of the

Saviour's death, extending in its saving power to the Patriarchs and Prophets, to Abel and Abraham, as well as to the apostles and to us. My simple purpose is to show that this difficulty, however it may arise, however it may be removed, is in harmony with other dispensations of God. If the gospel is not what men would have expected to find it, what men would have made it, in its *provisions*, no more is it in its *progress*. If it is alien from the natural apprehensions of men in its *substance*, it is alien to these apprehensions in its *development*. So that if it be inconsistent with the untutored anticipations of human reason, it is at least, throughout, and conspicuously consistent with itself, which is far better.

The principle alleged is comprehensive enough to apply to other difficulties, nearer and more pressing than this. It will apply to the future as well as the past; to the slow progress of love and light on the earth; not merely the introduction and existence, but the prevalence and persistency of sin and ignorance among the nations. This is a difficulty which thinking men cannot altogether evade. So far, indeed, as men are concerned, as the church is concerned, as *we* are concerned, alas! there is no difficulty in the case. The light of the gospel has shone so dimly, so feebly, over so scanty an area, because the proper light-bearers, light-dispensers, have been themselves so dark and so faithless; because instead of being themselves filled and glorified by this light, transfigured by its power, and translucent with its brightness, bearing it aloft and bearing it every where, it has been hidden under a bushel, it has been hardly able to shine obscurely out from the overlying mass of unbelief, and covetousness, and worldliness in ourselves, and we have done little and thought little to send it abroad. But in its relation to the sovereign dispensations of God, let us not be embarrassed or alarmed, but pray with increasing faith and fervency, "Thy kingdom come. Thy will be done on earth as it is in heaven;" and cry and sigh with Calvin, and other fervent saints, afflicted and cast down but not in despair, persecuted but not forsaken, "O Lord, how long? In the midst of the years make known, in wrath remember mercy."

The patience with which God now endures the reign of evil, the aspect and the character which the world bears under the dominion of Satan, is a standing trial of the believer's faith, and it is yet a majestic monument of the wisdom and grace of God, whose thoughts are not as our thoughts, and whose ways are not as our ways. All his schemes and movements are on a scale of infinite grandeur. With him a thousand years are as one day, and one day as a thousand years. Nothing can occur in the succession of times, and in the infinite variety of events and agents, to frustrate his purpose, or to disconcert his plans. All was foreseen, all was foreordained positively or permissively, and all will ultimately be overruled for the clearer manifestation of his own glory in the eternal salvation of his own children. Those very evils which now "perplex and dash our maturest counsels" will be found to work in most harmoniously with his concealed but cherished ends. When we contemplate these difficulties therefore, the part of wisdom is not to indulge scepticism, but to exercise faith, seeing they are in perfect keeping with the general plan and procedure of divine Providence. Let us be thankful for the gospel which, by bringing "life and immortality to light," scatters the darkness which would otherwise encompass his ways, and await with patience and hope the final "manifestation of the sons of God."

If the gospel be beyond the compass or the comprehension of nature, then it is evident that ministers should set it forth in all its simplicity, however repugnant to the notions or repulsive to the tastes of the natural man. It requires great faith to preach the gospel, as it ought to be preached. It requires spiritual discernment to perceive its spiritual glory and repose with unswerving confidence in its power to save. It is the simple truth that Jesus Christ came down from heaven to die for lost sinners that we must trust in, to be saved. Whosoever believeth in Jesus shall be saved; and the more simple the faith, the more child-like your trust in him, in his merit, his power, his grace, his perfect willingness to receive and bless all that come unto him and for his own name's sake to bestow upon them the Holy Spirit, the better. Luke xi. 13. Strange as it may seem, there are those in Christian lands who do not understand, and cannot be made to understand, the gospel of our salvation. They can repeat the Creed, the Ten Commandments, and give some tolerable account of the plan of salvation, and yet they do not truly, spiritually, practically, understand the gospel. They have never seen its spiritual beauty and glory. They have never beheld it from the true point of view. If they have seriously directed their eyes to this spiritual firmament, lit up with the highest splendours of the Father of lights, it has been as through an inverted telescope. They have never perceived the sovereign glory of God in the free forgiveness of guilty sinners, for the sake of Christ. Therefore, they have no sympathy with the grateful song of the redeemed in heaven: "Unto him that loved us and washed us in his own blood, and hath made us kings and priests unto God and the Father, unto him be glory and dominion for ever and ever, Amen."

It is surely not less evident, from the consideration of its transcendent nature, that a hearty acquiescence in the gospel doctrine is one of the plainest marks of saving grace, as the rejection of the gospel, though by men who are deeply religious according to their own scheme of salvation, is one of the saddest signs of final reprobation and ruin. When Dr. Archibald Alexander was about to die, and was looking for the last time for the evidence of his preparation for death, he tells us that he took a deliberate survey of the scheme of salvation offered in the Bible, and was conscious that he embraced it and could rest on it. This view of the subject, so purely objective and practical, might possibly simplify the enquiry to the mind of many a timid and doubtful disciple, conscious of much indwelling corruption, and embarrassed by artificial and minute tests of piety. We are sometimes confused by the multiplicity of the marks of a true faith which have been devised and recommended, and are discouraged because our own experience does not completely correspond with them. And when we search in the dark and dusty and winding passages of our own hearts, we cannot in many cases interpret our own spiritual state in a manner satisfactory to ourselves. They are too often indeed like the vineyard of the slothful, all grown over with thorns and briers, and the stone wall thereof overthrown, so that if there be the fair flower of grace in them and the fragrant fruits of righteousness, they are so covered over as to be well nigh, if not altogether, imperceptible. How comforting then to have a test so plain, so clear, in a sense so outward and open as this! Does my heart now fully acquiesce in this simple, scriptural method of salvation by the atoning sacrifice of the Lord Jesus? Does it seem to me all that is needed, and just what is needed? Do I let no other trust intrude, but simply take the offered gift, receive and rest upon the revealed Redeemer?

The substitution of external rites, though of divine origin, or any system of human philosophy, or an amalgamation of the two, for the pure gospel of the Son of God dying for our sins, is fatal to the soul. There is a deep seated disposition in human nature to depend upon something that men can do, instead of trusting simply and only to what Christ has done to save them. This is precisely what Paul charged upon the Jews. Rejecting the righteousness of God, they went about to establish their own righteousness, and so came short of the salvation of the gospel. We see the same evil leaven of will-worship and self-righteousness at work in unregenerate men now. They are impatient of unconditional submission to the authority of God, even as it is exercised in the dispensation of his grace. Allied to this is a secret tendency to substitute some system of human philosophy for the soul-humbling truths of revealed religion. Disgusted and confounded by the simplicity of the gospel method of salvation, they are tempted to exclaim with the proud Syrian, "Are not Abana and Pharpar, rivers of Damascus, better than all the waters of Israel? May I not wash in them and be clean?" and like him they are ready to go away in a rage. Now let me urge such with all solemnity to give heed to the simple doctrine of the gospel, to take the Saviour at his word, to renounce all trust in their own merit and strength, and as dying men, to look up to the living, gracious, interceding Saviour and live!

Since all the efforts even of the wisest men to devise a way of salvation for themselves have uniformly proved abortive, there is a clear obligation resting on the church to preach the gospel to every creature.

Shall we whose souls are lighted
With wisdom from on high—
Shall we to men benighted
The lamp of life deny?

It is surely a very remarkable fact that the Jews should have had so much more just and exalted apprehensions of religious truth than the Greeks—a nation otherwise incomparably more cultivated and intellectual. The only Jewish literature, of any account, is religious, and that is as far above the most famous productions of Grecian genius, as the inspired work of the eternal Spirit is above the native offspring of the human mind. Our first great duty to the world is to give it the gospel, as the one great want of the world is the knowledge of the gospel. Spread abroad then this pure, this mighty gospel. Wherever apostate man is found, let the saving grace of Christ be known. As you prize this blessed boon yourself, send it forth on the wings of the wind—to the ends of the earth.

LECTURE IV.

THE SENTIMENTAL AND THE SCRIPTURAL THEOLOGY.

THE paternal character of God is one in which we naturally delight to contemplate him. It is one which he does actually sustain toward the whole human race, as is clearly taught by the light of nature, and made still more certain by the authority of an inspired apostle, who quotes and adopts the sentiment of a Greek poet, "For we are also his offspring." Acts xvii. 28. There is unquestionably much in the varied and exuberant goodness of God, as we behold it in the forms of nature and in the facts of Providence, to beget filial confidence in the mind of a good man; but there is still enough, even in these, to dispel the notion of unmingled benevolence. God does, indeed, reveal himself in the endearing relation of a Father; but he is manifested not less clearly in the awful character of a Judge. Even in this world, there are painful events which show his righteousness, quite as impressively as any which proclaim his benevolence; and this, we should remember, is only a rudimentary, not a completed and final state. Hence, the tendencies of things are all that appear, the full consummation is reserved for eternity.

The general tendency of the light literature of the present day is to descant in soft and sentimental terms on the benevolence of God, which these writers represent as not only inexhaustible, but indiscriminate; in relation to his other attributes supreme and despotic, in relation to the objects of its exercise altogether irrespective of moral character. This favourite attribute they delight to honour, not only to the disparagement, but to the exclusion of his righteousness. To this end, they exalt certain pleasing facts and phenomena, and studiously keep out of view all of an opposite nature. Thus the God that has taken possession of the popular mind is not the God of the Bible; he is an easy, indulgent being, who disapproves of sin in his creatures, and has testified against it, but who will not be very rigorous in its punishment.

Such views savour rather of romance than reality, and correspond rather with the wishes than the experience of men. In nature, God appears not only in the sunny and smiling landscape, but in the tornado and tempest. He not only sends fruitful seasons, filling our hearts with food and gladness, but gaunt famine, wasting pestilence, blighting mildew. We see the triumphal chariot, but it is met by the funeral hearse. We hear the voice of mirth and revelry, but if we listen for a moment, we shall hear notes of sadness and fear. Laughter is followed by a sigh. We can scarcely enjoy our present possessions, from the dread that we shall lose them. The beauty, which we gaze on with joy to-day, to-morrow may be laid in the grave. The labour of years may be destroyed by the forgetfulness of an hour. The inheritance of many generations may be lost by the heedlessness of a servant, or an accidental spark, or an unexpected flood. The world, in which we live, is subject to decay and change. Our life-long friend may betray or forsake us. Slander may blacken our names, and those we love as our own souls may be smitten by death. Sorrow is written on every human countenance, in characters which none can mistake. The most happy on earth are only the least miserable.

There may be beings in the universe, toward whom the infinite Author of all manifests himself in the tenderness of a purely paternal character; because, toward them, there may be no occasion for the vindication of rights which have never been invaded, or the enforcement of claims which have never been disputed. But not thus assuredly does he manifest himself toward us, who have been guilty of such foul revolt. Toward us, he reveals himself in the awful terrors of injured justice, of outraged and indignant majesty.

Now, we experience an alternation of good and ill; of joy and sorrow; of pain and pleasure; of health and sickness; of life to be followed by, to end with, to be swallowed up in death. Our earthly condition is not simple but mixed; our earthly experience is not a complete and consistent whole, but fragmentary and imperfect; not homogeneous, not of a piece, but contradictory and conflicting. We are rarely well, even in body; not merely free altogether from pain, but in a state of positive bodily enjoyment, in which the very sense of existence is a conscious delight. And if the body be diseased and partially disabled, in the mind of every man there is a certain unsoundness. Each man has his own particular folly; his constitutional infirmity; his besetting sin. Heb. xii. 1. On some subjects and to some extent we are all insane, or have been; we may have sense enough for ordinary purposes, but pure reason and perfect knowledge we have not. We seek it, but it for ever eludes our grasp, as flies from our approach like the horizon; or in mathematics, two lines approach each other for ever, and never touch; or in natural philosophy, our hypothetical estimates are never absolutely exact, and we must make some allowance for friction and rigidity of cordage. Ignorance and error encompass the very wisest men in relation to the most important matters.

There are those, who make it a matter of ostentatious boast, that they fear not God, and regard it as the mark of a weak and craven spirit to fear him. But who is this dreadful God? And who are these puny creatures who presume to despise and defy him? He is the great and dreadful God; mighty in counsel and excellent in working, who planted the pillars of the earth, and can remove them out of their places, who giveth to all men life and breath and all things, in whose hand our breath is, and whose are all our ways, who appointeth the moon for seasons and whose sun knoweth his going down, who doth his will among the armies of heaven and among the inhabitants of the earth, who turneth man to destruction and saith, "Return ye children of men." "Who knoweth the power of thine anger? even according to thy fear so is thy wrath;" Ps. xc. 11. "Who would not fear thee, O King of nations? for unto thee doth it appertain." Jer. x. 7. And who is man that he should dare to contemn the wrath of the Almighty? The creature of a day, a worm of the dust, crushed before the moth, liable to instant death, from an invisible insect or atom; dependent for his continued existence on the gracious energy of that awful Being, whom he so audaciously provokes. Of all the follies that men on the earth commit, the most fruitful and fatal is to cast off the fear of God.

So far as it regards the insult offered to the divine Majesty, and the injury which they themselves sustain, it is perfectly immaterial whether this insane confidence is built on the belief that God is unable or that he is unwilling to punish them. Of one class it is true that they are like the Sadducees of old, not knowing the Scriptures nor the power of God. The other class attribute to the God of truth and righteousness the same insensibility to sin which they find in themselves, and he might truly address them in the language of the prophet Asaph, "Thou thoughtest that I was altogether such a one as thyself; but I will reprove thee and set them in order before thine eyes." Ps. l. 21.

Upon no subject are men prone to fall into more serious and hurtful error, than in regard to what they imagine suitable to the character of God. Losing sight of that pure and glorious Being whom the Bible reveals to our faith and worship, they form in their foolish hearts, a God like themselves. This has always been the disposition of corrupt mankind. It was so in the time of the Apostle Paul. It is so now. Then they turned the truth of God into a lie; *i. e.*, they exchanged the true God for a false one. They could not behold his holiness and truth, without self-condemnation and alarm; and therefore they divested him of these attributes in their thoughts and adapted the service which they offered him, not to his majesty and excellence, but to the erroneous and degrading conceptions which they had formed of his nature. Thus they disrobed him of his real and essential glories, and arrayed him in false and imaginary perfections. So we find in our own day that there are men who profess unlimited veneration for the divine character; representing themselves as his only true and worthy worshippers; declaring that all who assert his punitive justice do dishonour to his nature, and make him out a cruel and sanguinary tyrant, exulting in the eternal agonies of his hapless offspring. While affecting to honour God, they are heaping upon him the foulest indignity. While in words magnifying his mercy and grace, they in fact strip him of holiness, justice, and truth. They array our Lord in purple and put a sceptre in his hands, but it is in mockery and scorn. They seem to surpass his most devoted followers in expressions of reverence and esteem, but the only tendency of their caresses is to betray and to crucify. They impiously affirm that God is too merciful to visit the transgressions of a finite and fallible creature with everlasting woe. Miserable men! how fatal the delusion in which you are held captive! When was God too merciful to punish sin unrepented, unforsaken, unforgiven, with banishment for ever from his favour and presence? Where now are those rebel angels, who dared to wage impious battle against the King of heaven? In uncontrollable and endless torment! When shall the sound of release or remission gladden their hearts? Never! If it was not inconsistent with the mercy of God to inflict such punishment on sinful angels, why should he not inflict it on sinful men? Have angels not been as much exalted and blessed? Are they not capable of as deep degradation and pain? If God has pitied and loved with such amazing tenderness, be assured he will take destructive vengeance. If he has at any time made stupendous displays of his grace, be assured he will make equally stupendous exhibitions of his judgments. For all the actions and attributes of Jehovah have a grandeur commensurate with his divine nature.

When these sophistical and sentimental objectors come into the atmosphere of the Bible, their respiration is uneasy and imperfect. The God whose voice is heard in every sentence, and whose image is reflected on every page, is not the God of their imagination and affections. He is to them a strange God. The commonest words of the New Testament, holiness, righteousness, grace, inspire unconquerable disgust. The aspect under which they view God, is one adapted to divest him of every attribute which might excite terror. They throw an impenetrable veil over those exhibitions of his character, which render him an object of apprehension to sinners, and bring forward in bold relief every thing tending to allay alarm, and beget a profane and pernicious confidence.

Now it is undeniable, that God has a controversy with the whole human race. Under the existing economy, man is born to trouble as the sparks fly upwards. There are terrible visitations abroad in the earth. Men suffer under every form of pain, calamity, and disease. We all come into the world convicts under a sentence of death. We enjoy a brief respite, which is continually interrupted by painful monitions of our mortal state. The representations of the word of God on this subject exactly accord with the actual experience of man, wherever found, whatever his country, climate, laws, government, religion, or race. Turning away from those who are ready to lie for God, to prophesy smooth things, to prophesy deceits, to the sure testimonies of God himself, all is perfectly intelligible; the dispensations of his providence and the testimonies of his word are seen and felt to be in absolute harmony. In the Scriptures, the real relations which subsist between Him who is at once the Father of mercies and a God of righteousness, and his rebellious children, shine forth in the unchanging and awful light of truth. In them, the infinite goodness of God is not more distinctly affirmed than his unspotted holiness. In them, the feelings, with which God once regarded man, and with which man once regarded God, are spoken of as having undergone a corresponding change, and given place to others of mutual estrangement.

There are in every climate, in every object, traces of the severity and the goodness, the wrath and the kindness of God. The contradiction of mute, material nature, is just what we might expect it to be, under the righteous government of the God of revelation. The double aspect of earthly things caused the ancient Gnostics and Manichaeans to feign two Gods, a supreme and a subordinate, a benevolent and a malignant deity; and modern sceptics have been often driven to atheism by the apparent uncertainty, confusion, and disorder, which we find in the world of nature. The same ray of sunlight, which ripens the growing grain, darts contagious fire—pours raging fever into the blood of the husbandman, who fondly hoped to enjoy the mature fruits of his labours. There is the deadly hemlock growing beside the healing balm; now the desolating torrent, and now the fragrant and gentle shower; the tremendous concussions of nature, and the soft landscape sleeping in the moonlight, and bathed in the dew. There is here the festive gathering, but it crosses the slow-moving funeral train. In one house, there is a gay wedding, and in the next street, a mother with heart-wrung anguish is bending over the couch of her pale, unconscious, dying child. Again, there is the voice of infant mirth, ringing out clear and glad, and the old man sobbing in desolate agony, and looking to the grave as his only friend.

The influences which tend to steep men in spiritual slumber, derive much of their power from their speciousness and subtlety. They are connected with a partial view of the character and providence of God. They come dressed in the fascinating garb of sentiment and poetry. There is so much of truth mingled with them, and they apparently render such willing and splendid homage to the goodness of our heavenly Father, and present him to the imagination in an attitude so winning, that to oppose the error seems almost impious. And yet the error is only the more mischievous because it is thus disguised.

We shall never truly honour God by exalting one attribute at the expense of another, or by the contemplation of one to the exclusion of another. Truth, in all things, and especially in regard to God, will be found ultimately to be not only the safest, but the most truly beautiful. There are stern and solemn facts daily taking place before our eyes, which should arouse us from these illusive dreams. There are scenes of wretchedness around us, which we can no more explain than we can deny, except on the concession that God is not made up of benevolence, unaccompanied by attributes of a more severe kind. What means that bed of straw on which the pallid sufferer has been lying for years, with pain which time has only increased? When by these means, the person is brought to piety and to heaven, or receives any material moral benefit, we can understand it; and the advantage is greatly on the side of the sufferer. The physic, though bitter, has wrought a cure. The road, though rough, has led to the much loved home. The voyage, though stormy, has ended in the desired haven. This consideration should sustain God's afflicted children. "No suffering for the present seemeth to be joyous, but grievous; nevertheless afterward it yieldeth the peaceable fruits of righteousness in them which are exercised thereby." But is this the case with all? Are there none who suffer severely at the hand of God, and who suffer without profit, without repentance, and without contrition? It cannot be doubted that there are such persons. This is a painful case to contemplate. But it is necessary to a view of the whole truth, and it may prove more useful than a more pleasing train of observation. It proves that punishment is not always disciplinary, even in this world; that there are cases, in which it is evidently and only retributive. This we are assured by inspiration is the essential nature and proper end of future punishment. It is for the vindication of God's justice, not to illustrate his benevolence.

There are those who flatly deny all this, who represent God as sustaining exclusively a paternal character toward men; and who thus quell the rising fears of their own consciences, and the salutary apprehensions of others. Now for the effectual conviction of such men, and to dispel the perilous error in which they are involved—it is necessary to pass in review a class of facts, which it is very painful to consider. We are compelled to contemplate God, not only as he sits enthroned in smiling goodness over his glad and grateful creatures; opening his hand and satisfying the desire of every living thing, and therefore, an object of trust and of tenderness; but likewise as making his power known by present demonstrations of destroying vengeance against the workers of iniquity; and therefore, a God not only to be loved but to be feared. He has not only denounced for the future, but inflicted before our eyes, indignation and wrath, tribulation and anguish, upon every soul of man that doeth evil. "Upon the wicked, he shall rain snares, fire and brimstone, and a horrible tempest; this shall be the portion of their cup." Ps. xi. 6. Ought not men to consider the solemn facts and calls of God's providence? Ought they not to fear him? Are not the most terrible denunciations of what he will do in eternity, of the intolerable weight of his wrath which shall finally break forth and bear down and burn to the lowest hell—borne out by the plain proofs of his consuming indignation against the children of disobedience, which he has afforded, even in this world? But the uncompromising and inviolable sacredness of the law, which these presumptuous despisers spurn, is seen, most of all, in the gracious method by which the voice which cried for the blood of the sinner is silenced by the blood of the Saviour. The character of Jehovah must be inflexible in its righteousness, when his well-beloved Son must drain to the dregs the bitter cup of anguish, simply because he stood in the sinner's place and sustained what infinite justice adjudged to the sinner's substitute. The ground of carnal security is a false view of the moral character and the moral government of God. Men could not remain careless in their sins, if they seriously believed and thought upon the truth. It is not in the nature of things. It is not in the nature of man.

Let us now proceed to point out the moral use

and bearing of this argument. An objector may affirm that these views of God—of the objects, the means, and the ends of his moral government, are derogatory to his benevolence. The reply is obvious: explain them as you can; deny them if you will; still they are experimentally true. We cannot be more satisfied of our own existence, than of these facts and principles of the divine administration. But we take higher ground. They are not only true, but they are honourable to God. Those who deny or asperse them, degrade while they pretend to exalt him. While they profess to be contending for the honour of his name, they rob him of his most sacred and shining glories. These pains, proceeding as they do from the presence of sin, proclaim more loudly than a voice from heaven his holy abhorrence of sin. By these dreadful terrors and solemn sanctions is the unspotted righteousness of his eternal throne vindicated. They are not only designed to impress the mind with salutary awe—to instruct us in regard to the insufferable odiousness of sin, and so to deter us and others from the commission of it, and allure us onward to holiness and heaven—they have an additional and a more awful purpose in view. We can have nothing like an adequate apprehension of the terrors of the Almighty, and conscience is disarmed of her most dreaded sting, while we yield ourselves to the imagination so assiduously cherished by a superficial and sentimental theology, that the only design of punishment is disciplinary; that in all cases in which pain is endured, the purpose is either to reform the sufferer, or to warn others. There is, under the government of God, a retributive justice which marks its power and makes its presence known, in the sufferings of the guilty, not only in this world, but in that which is to come.

The view presented throws a painful but a powerful light on the doctrine of human depravity. It shows that it is no pedantic dogma about which bigotted theologians may wrangle, with the consideration of which men of sense and candour have nothing to do. It shows that as this appalling corruption is present in the experience of every man, so it is a fact, which has materially affected every man's relations towards God. So that, if it be ignored, no great question in morals can be understood or settled aright. So interwoven is it with our recollections, our experience, and our prospects; so essentially does it modify the feelings, with which we are regarded, and the principles on which we are treated, on the part of God, that it is a material element in the solution of every problem, which respects the relations of the creature to the Creator. Why this extensive suffering in the universe of God? Why pain, sickness, death? Because of sin. The existence of sin is an ultimate fact. When we have pushed our inquiries to this point we must stop short. Beyond this, revelation is silent, and reason and experience cannot pass. To those who deny either the righteousness of God or the sinfulness of men, and the binding link between them, the actual experience of the human race must be an inexplicable enigma.

There is nothing which the Bible discloses, in relation to the condition of man in a future world, which we do not behold in principle, in seed, and in germ, in our present economy. The government now carried on is not the perfection of moral government; but still it is truly moral. There is the native impression on every unsophisticated mind, that vice deserves to be punished, not simply for the good of the offender or for the benefit of others, but simply because it is vice. God has himself distinctly announced this fact, in our present constitution, in the uneasiness or pleasure which arises in the mind, according as we have done what we regard as a good or a bad action. Thus we have the fact of moral rewards and punishments, established in the most immediate and intimate manner. Could we receive the infallible assurance, that no human being would ever be injured by what we had done amiss, and did we know that there was no possibility of its repetition by ourselves; still if we distinctly recognized it as wrong, we should quite as distinctly recognize it as worthy of punishment; and the pungency and the power of this conviction, would be in precise proportion to the moral sensibility and purity of the offender. The man whose moral feelings and whose moral judgments were most like God's, would have the most oppressive sense of guilt, if consciously a sinner.

These are plain traces of a righteous government, whence it is easy to answer all objections, since they proceed from, and imply a righteous Governor. It is the highest evidence that God approves righteousness and abhors sin, that he has made his vicegerent and voice in the soul, to testify with such authority on the side of righteousness. The conscience of the human race is the moral vindicator of God. He has inserted in the breast of every living man a principle and a power, that bears instant witness to the infinite rectitude of the divine character, and the inviolate justice of God, in his fearful visitations on the lawless and disobedient. The office of conscience is two-fold: to guide man and testify for God. The profoundest interpretation of its utterances is given by the smitten and penitent psalmist when he says, "That thou mightest be justified when thou speakest and be clear when thou judgest." Ps. li. 4. In the present life, men may sport themselves with their own deceivings, resolutely shutting their eyes to the manifold traces of a righteous government all around them, refusing to acknowledge the God either of Scripture or of Providence, and making to themselves an imaginary being who will verily clear the guilty, that they may cast off all fear and sin, as it were with a cart-rope. But let such remember that God has made ample provision, not only for the execution but for the vindication of his righteous sentence. What shall at last be spoken by the voice of the eternal Judge, shall be echoed by the conscience of the condemned. The circumstance, of all others, which will render that sentence most fearful, is that it will be felt to be just. "And a voice came out of the throne, saying, Praise our God all ye his servants, and ye that fear him both small and great. And I heard, as it were, the voice of a great multitude, and as the voice of many waters, and as the voice of a mighty thundering, saying, Alleluia: for the Lord God omnipotent reigneth." Rev. xix. 5, 6. "I have sworn by myself, the word is gone out of my mouth in righteousness, and shall not return, That unto me every knee shall bow and every tongue shall swear." Isa. xlv. 23. "Those mine enemies which would not that I should reign over them, bring hither and slay them before me." Luke xix. 27.

It plainly appears from the unchangeable character of God, and from the feelings with which he now regards sinners, that they are shut up to the salvation of the gospel. The appalling dispensations of his providence, which now so expressively mark his purpose to punish sin, are only the premonitions of a more overwhelming perdition which will be the eternal portion of the finally impenitent. God, out of Christ, is a consuming fire. But God sent not his Son into the world to condemn the world, but that the world through him might be saved. The sum of the gospel testimony, is that

"God was in Christ reconciling the world unto himself; not imputing their trespasses unto them." Let such therefore as think the view of the divine character and government, presented in this chapter, harsh and repulsive, know that it is inseparably connected with our pardon, peace, and safety. We seek merely to drive them from a deceitful trust, that their feet may rest upon a solid rock. The same principle of immutable righteousness, which secures the condemnation of the impenitent, is pledged for the salvation of the believer in Jesus. Just as the man who rejects the salvation of the gospel, through unbelief, will be sentenced to everlasting perdition by the unchanging fiat of Jehovah, so the man who believes on the Son of God, "shall not perish but have everlasting life." John iii. 16. For the salvation of the believer, we have all the assurance that can arise from all the attributes of God; from all the dispensations of providence; from all the promises of the gospel, and from all the provisions of heavenly glory. Rom. viii. 28; John xiv. 2. The way of access, the new and living way, has been opened to the favour of God, and the ripe fruits of that favour in the paradise above. "Having therefore, brethren, boldness to enter into the holiest by the blood of Jesus, by a new and living way which he hath consecrated for us, through the veil, that is to say, his flesh; and having a high priest over the house of God, let us draw near with a true heart, in full assurance of faith, having our hearts sprinkled from an evil conscience and our bodies washed with pure water." Heb. x. 19–22. The acceptance of the man who relies not on his own works but on the grace of God; who, casting away every other ground of trust, reposes on the word of God, and receives with humble thankfulness the great salvation; is secured by the very righteousness, which adjudges the obstinate sinner to everlasting woe. It is likewise on the same basis that the accepted believer may triumphantly rest for the effectual keeping of that which he has committed to his faithful Saviour. They whom the Father hath given to Christ, in eternity, and who, constrained by his grace, have given themselves to him in time, are kept by the power of God, through faith unto salvation. The righteousness of God, which is the ground of just dread to the man who persists in his sins, is the refuge and bulwark of the man who has fled for refuge to the hope set before him.

Religious reverence makes up a large part of intelligent and acceptable piety. God is the object of humble adoration to the heavenly hosts. How much more lowly the homage, due the Majesty on high, from guilty creatures, such as we! Wherever God has revealed himself to men, he has surrounded himself with circumstances of majesty and terror, clouds and darkness, lightnings and thunderings. Thus he appeared to Moses and Isaiah; to Ezekiel and to Daniel; to Paul and to John; and thus he will appear to every eye, in the awful Epiphany of the last day!

The Apostle draws a distinction, however, to which it becomes us to give heed. It is that which obtains between a reverential and a servile fear. The one is the feeling of an affectionate son for an honoured father. The other, that of a sullen slave for an abhorred and dreaded lord. The right faith and the right fear draw men near to God in holy fellowship and in willing service. They make men fearful of committing sin, which is that evil and bitter thing that God hates. They render his favour which is life, and his loving-kindness which is better than life, the object of supreme desire and delight. This is that fear of the Lord, which makes men depart from evil. It is that fear of the Lord which is the beginning of wisdom; and which, so far from being lessened, is increased with growth in knowledge and grace. A servile and sinful fear, on the other hand, is founded on the conviction of guilt, and the absence of faith in the mercy of God and in the merit of Christ, our most gracious Mediator and Advocate. Its effect is to fill the soul with hostility and bitterness, and render the thought of drawing near to God intolerable. It is the feeling which sprang up in the remorseful soul of apostate Adam, and is displaced by a delightful confidence, when the painful sense of guilt has been exchanged for a heartfelt trust in the grace of Immanuel! A servile and sinful dread is the perennial source of all will-worship and superstition. A godly and filial reverence is the fountain whence issue the streams which make glad the city of our God, free and joyful worship, grateful and holy obedience. The one is the spirit of popery; the other, the spirit of the true gospel church.

LECTURE V.

RELATION OF REASON TO REVELATION.

In the revealed word there is, as it were, a re-appearing of the original Paradise of God; in which there is the greatest abundance of trees, good for food and fair to look upon, of which we may freely eat; and others kept in sacred seclusion—"a privacy of glorious light"—a religious reserve not to be violated without sin and death.

There are certain disclosures of revelation, which belong to us just as truly as the permitted trees of the garden belonged to Adam; truths as beautiful, as grand, as precious, as the immortal fruits and flowers that shed fragrance and beauty and endless riches there:

> Groves of myrrh,
> And flowering odours, cassia, nard, and balm,
> A wilderness of sweets.

In the Bible are revelations touching the nature, the purposes, and the empire of God; setting forth the origin, the fall, and the redemption of man—the creation, the government, and the destiny of this material Universe, to all of which we have as free access as Adam had to any of the trees of Eden. While there are truths relating to all these matters, but more immediately pertaining to the nature and purposes of God, as inaccessible, as veiled in the unfathomable mysteries of his providence, as were any of the trees of the garden, to which we have no more right to draw near than Adam had to taste of the tree of the knowledge of good or evil—or the people of Bethshemesh to gaze with profane eyes into the Ark of God—or any other than the high priest among the Hebrews to enter in and examine the awful arcana of the Holy of Holies.

There is this difference, however, that Adam was at liberty to eat or not to eat of the permitted fruits. We have no such liberty. We are positively required, on pain of the sore displeasure of Almighty God, to search diligently into the things that are revealed. I hardly know which is the greater sin, to pry into the unrevealed or to slight the revealed mind of God. Certain it is, that the things which are revealed are not only our property but our province. It is not only our right but our duty to know and do all the revealed will of God. On the same authority, and to the same degree, we are bound not to be wise *above* what is written; and to be sure that we are wise *up to* what is written. The revelation of God is to be the measure of our knowledge and faith. In the whole compass of the Bible, there is not one revealed truth of which we may remain innocently or safely ignorant. There is no folly into which men fall, or sin that they commit, against which they are not guarded in Scripture; and which they might not have escaped, had they given intelligent heed to the sure testimonies of God. "Thy word," says David, "have I hid in my heart, that I might not sin against thee." "Wherewith shall a young man cleanse his way? by taking heed thereto according to thy word." "All Scripture is given by inspiration of God, and is profitable for doctrine, for reproof, for correction, for instruction in righteousness." Ps. cxix. 11, 9; 2 Tim. iii. 16. No portion of the Scripture can be safely overlooked or underrated. All is needful. All is useful. Every part is inspired, and the whole binding on the conscience.

If there be one truth revealed in the Bible, and that truth be one of which we remain in willing ignorance—that one truth may belong to the law or the gospel—it may set in array the terrors of the Almighty, or it may be full of grace—and yet, contrary to its own nature and proper tendency, it may become to us the occasion of death; first, by way of privation and absence. It may be the very truth that we need for correction, for consolation, for reproof, or for instruction in righteousness. Or secondly, by way of direct and positive operation. It may be a word of grace, but that word is turned against us, and becomes to us a word of death, like the sword which is madly directed against the bosom it should have defended. The truths of

God's word are like the pillar of cloud that went before ancient Israel; they have a bright side and a dark; they are a light and defence to his friends; obscurity and terror to his foes.

Lord Bacon says, "The prerogative of God extendeth as well to the reason as to the will of man; so that as we are to obey his law, though we find a reluctation in our will, so we are to believe his word, though we find a reluctation in our reason." There is hardly any subject of inquiry more difficult and important, than the true limits and use of reason in spiritual things. It is the office of reason to weigh *the evidence* of what purports to be a revelation from God; and we cannot be too cautious or too exact in our examination of what claims to be of supernatural origin and of binding authority. But when once adequately attested, all that remains to reason, the proper and the only function of reason, is not to determine beforehand, what such revelation can consistently unfold, but simply to ascertain with all available helps and, above all, with humble prayer to the eternal Spirit, what it actually discloses.

It is no business of ours to reconcile the several doctrines of the Bible with one another. There is, no doubt, an interior, though it may be, for the present, an invisible harmony between them; and hereafter, doubtless, all apparent discrepancies will be resolved into a higher unity. We are not bound to evince the logical consistency, for instance, between divine sovereignty and human responsibility, the election of God and the free agency of man. The one is assumed, the other affirmed throughout the Scriptures. The one is necessary to the constitution of man, the other to the authority of God. The one is an intimate and universal fact of consciousness, the other is an essential and inalienable prerogative of God. Without the one, we cease to be men; without the other, he ceases to be God. Without the one, we should not be capable of salvation; without the other, there could be no salvation for us. In a word, every man feels that he is responsible to God for what he is, and dependent upon God for what he should be. So true is that saying of Augustine, "Command what thou wilt, and give what thou dost command."

It is the height of folly for men to torment themselves about the secret decrees of the Most High. They never can know them. They never were designed to be known but by the event, or the plain prognostic of the event. The eternal election or reprobation of particular persons, belongs to this class of truths. Many assume, always without authority, and often most erroneously, that they are non-elect, that God never designed to save them, that if he did, he will save them without any anxiety or exertion on their part; and therefore, they fold their hands in total apathy, awaiting some extraordinary visitation of the Holy Ghost, without offering that prayer which is at once a proof of his presence and a pledge of his favour. Now what may be the secret purpose of God in regard to any particular individual, is wholly unknown to himself or to any other human being: and of course, it should not, in reason, be the motive or the rule of his personal action. If secret, if unrevealed, it is that with which we can have no direct concern. It is not an element of responsibility or a rule of action to us. But "the word is nigh thee, even in thy mouth and in thy heart: that is, the word of faith which we preach: That if thou shalt confess with thy mouth the Lord Jesus, and shalt believe in thine heart that God hath raised Him from the dead, thou shalt be saved. For with the heart man believeth unto righteousness, and with the mouth confession is made unto salvation." Rom. x. 8—10.

How unreasonable and sinful is it, then, for men to be perplexing themselves about the secret decrees of God, and the ultimate issue of things, when the way of salvation is so plainly pointed out in the Scriptures, when the only condition exacted is a sense of need and a free acceptance of everlasting life! Any man, who is willing to be saved on these terms, God, for Christ's sake, is willing to save! and he is willing to save no man on any other terms. This is positively all that is revealed concerning the purpose of God toward any. He does not say of any particular sinner, that he is elect or non-elect. He says of some, "Ye will not come unto me that ye might have life." He says to all,

"Come unto me all ye that are weary and heavy-laden and I will give you rest." "And if any man thirst, let him come unto me and drink."

The secret things of God are a stumbling-block, over which many souls fall into perdition. It may be that some of my young readers may be "throwing their inch of time away," in endless and profitless endeavour to find out what is not revealed, and what can be known only from the event, or from those spiritual fruits, which are the effects of grace, and therefore the presages of glory. The most favoured and mature Christian can know his gracious election of God only by inference. There is no private and special revelation to any of his eternal designation in the purpose of God to have a part in the glorious inheritance of the saints in light. Even the Apostles when upon the earth were saved by hope; that is, their salvation in its complete consummation was prospective, not present; a matter of anticipation, not a matter of experience. The true and the right process is this. We rise from the consciousness of love to God to the conclusion that he loves us—for we know from the Scripture that if we love him, it is only because he first loved us. We are sensible of being the subjects of holy dispositions, sympathies, desires; and we know that all who are the subjects of such affections, and who bring forth such fruits, are ordained unto eternal life. Hence the exquisite beauty and fitness of Archbishop Leighton's comparison of the decree of election to a golden chain let down from heaven to earth: the centre link, holiness, being within the sight of men, and the two extremes, eternal election and eternal glory, reserved in the keeping of God.

The Lord has revealed his will so far as it is needful for us to know it, but he has disclosed nothing for the gratification of mere curiosity or carnal speculation. We should be concerned therefore to explore the counsels of the Most High only so far as he has been pleased to make them known. He has inculcated modesty upon us, in all our religious inquiries, by making it the indispensable condition of true knowledge, as well as in the method and measure of his gracious communications.

Profound and insoluble difficulties present themselves in the infancy of thought, and in every subsequent stage of our intellectual progress. They startle the child as well as the man; the savage as well as the philosopher; and their satisfactory solution is as effectually hidden from one as from the other.

Thus to take the fundamental difficulty of all—the existence anywhere in the universe of God, of any sort of evil moral or physical, for any period extended or brief. This is a difficulty by no means peculiar to the Christian Scriptures or to the Christian system, but pertaining as well to every other scheme of religion and philosophy. The existence of evil is a fact that confronts the Atheist as palpably and broadly as it does the Bible believer. It is a fact which is simply recognized as a fact under every dispensation. It is not accounted for, not vindicated; but assumed or asserted in every part of Scripture. Still the specific and perfect method by which it is to be reconciled with the attributes of God, is nowhere intimated—the reasons which determined a Being of infinite wisdom, power, and goodness to permit it, are not even glanced at—a profound darkness envelopes the whole subject; and every attempt which men have made to dissipate the darkness has served only to make it more palpably obscure.

As a matter of fact, the associated doctrines of original sin and total depravity are painfully attested by the universal history of our race. How different would the present aspect of the world be, if, from the beginning of time until now, men had employed the thought, the money, and the effort in advancing the physical and intellectual well-being of one another, their progress in knowledge, virtue, and happiness, which they have expended in mutual slaughter, persecution, and ruin! The greatest of all mysteries calls for the exercise of the greatest faith, and so of all lesser mysteries in their degree. We are divinely assured that the whole scheme of things was not suddenly improvised on an unexpected emergency; but foreseen and foreordained from all eternity, for the highest conceivable end, the most illustrious display of the divine perfections.

It is expressly affirmed that it is his sublime prerogative to bring good out of evil; and in the events connected with our Redeemer's advent, life, and death, in their remote relations and revealed results, we have the clearest demonstration of this cheering truth.

It has been an occasion of astonishment, and perhaps of infidelity to some, that God should have visited sin, under the old dispensation, with such destructive judgments; as in the case of Sodom, of Korah, of Achan, and others. The true solution, undoubtedly, is that at that time the doctrines of a future state and eternal punishment were obscurely revealed; and the most appalling instance of his wrath against sin had not then been exhibited in the unparalleled sufferings of his beloved Son. The Mosaic Dispensation was especially designed to illustrate the holiness of God: the Christian, his grace.

If sin be a greater evil than pain, as every one not utterly debased will admit, then the pains of life consequent on sin, and designed to punish and prevent it, so far from being in conflict with the wisdom and goodness of God, are a strong confirmation of both. That there should be suffering in this life, therefore, admitting the existence of sin, presents no mystery to reason, and should create no difficulty or surprise; but should be considered inevitable, under the government of God, and on the hypothesis of sin. Suffering is the frown of God on sin. It is as natural, considering who God is, and what sin is, as the darkening of the day when the beautiful sunlight is obscured by an intervening cloud, or as the face of a wise and loving father is shaded with displeasure at the presence or mention of an undutiful son. The most signal mark of God's favour indeed is the making its object holy, though by a painful process. How could a human friend show such friendship as by seeking to lead us to holiness, though by a rough and thorny path; and how could God show his larger love more wisely than by effecting the same gracious end, though by piercing sorrows? The advanced Christian will value the gifts of God's grace above those of his providence, and will therefore take joyfully the spoiling of his goods, the loss of his health, or the death of his friends, if it yield the peaceable fruits of righteousness to himself or others.

The sufferings of infants and saints are mysterious; but what if we had seen the Son of God taunted, buffeted, expiring on the cross! Let the believer then think of the sorrows of his Lord, when his own seem mysterious. Let him ponder the death of his Saviour, when his own death seems dreadful. There is profound wisdom in the saying of John Howe, that no secrets of nature can outvie the mysteries of godliness.

The reason why particular events in time have occurred at one period rather than another, is in many cases unsearchable by the human understanding. It is one of God's secrets. It is locked up by the King of kings in his cabinet councils; not offered to the gaze of created intelligences. Dr. Arnold, a wise observer of the ways of providence as revealed in the history of nations, remarks in his Lectures on Modern History: "No man can say why the great discoveries of science were made only at the time and in the country when and where they were made actually: why the compass was withheld from the navigation of the Roman empire, but was already in existence, when it was needed to aid the genius of Columbus: why printing was invented in time to preserve that portion of Greek literature which still survived in the fifteenth century, but was not known early enough to prevent the irreparable mischiefs of the Latin storming of Constantinople in the thirteenth: why the steam engine, triumphing over time and space, was denied to the striving spirit of the sixteenth century, and reserved to display its wonderful works only to the nineteenth."

These are only a few samples of innumerable questions of the same general character, which may be asked, but which cannot be satisfactorily answered. "What I do," says Christ to Peter, "thou knowest not now, but thou shalt know hereafter." All the dispensations of God toward nations, families, and individuals, which are not interpreted in the event, will be intelligible in eternity. No cloud will ultimately rest on the character of

God, as Ruler and Judge. The set time for the full vindication of his ways, is the judgment of the great day. Then, doubtless, all seeming incongruities will be reconciled; all obscurities cleared up; and the sun of his righteousness shine forth with unclouded ray. Then, satisfied, thankful, joyful, all his saints shall sing the song of Moses and the Lamb, saying, "Great and marvellous are thy words, Lord God Almighty; just and true are thy ways, thou king of saints!" Rev. xv. 3, 4.

As in the ancient dispensation, before the coming of Christ, many types and usages might have seemed unmeaning and even absurd, which are now clear and significant; so in the future world many things may be seen to be wise and righteous in the economy of God, which at present we cannot understand. We must be content, therefore, to walk by faith, not by sight. Faith in God is the great cure alike for the maladies of human nature, and the infirmities of human reason. The predominance of sense is one of the most comprehensive evils of the fall. Faith is opposed to sense and not to reason; so far as it prevails it subdues the one and exalts the other, cheering the desponding soul by the promised rewards of the celestial paradise. Faith in the full disclosures of eternity, in regard to the profound mysteries which prevail in the two grand departments of providence and grace, should inspire patience. Now we are in darkness; but then we shall know, even as we are known. Now our discoveries of truth are slow, circuitous, obscure, and partial; then they will be rapid, intuitive, clear, and perfect.

Human reason can no more comprehend the whole compass of divine revelation, than the human eye can take in, at a glance, the whole material universe. Therefore, let us cease from man whose breath is in his nostrils, even the wisest, the greatest, and the best, and let us look to God as our infallible Teacher and sovereign Lord.

It is not surprising that men should find difficulties in Scripture, who, in addition to the ordinary infirmities of human reason, read it in a spirit so different from that in which it was written by the holy men of old. Having nothing in their own spiritual experience to correspond with its sacred truths, and no proper sympathy with them, they can have no true knowledge, no adequate appreciation of them. To enjoy the beauties of nature, of literature, and of art, requires delicate sensibility, and a cultivated taste. How much more to discern and delight in the spiritual splendors which light up the firmament of inspired Scripture! 1 Cor. ii. 14. It is true not only of individuals, but of whole generations, that when frivolous, heartless, sensual, and blood-thirsty, they have been invariably sceptical in regard to divine revelation, and prone to reject it.

It belongs to the sovereignty of God to determine first, whether he shall give to us a supernatural revelation of his will at all; secondly, what the revelation shall unfold, and what it shall conceal; what portion of the spiritual horizon it shall illuminate, and what it shall leave in partial or in total darkness. In other words, the fact, the matter, the measure, and the methods of divine revelation, all pertain alike and alone to the sovereignty of God, who at one time hideth himself in the majesty of darkness, and at another covereth himself with light, as with a garment—of whom, at one time, it is said, his pavilion round about him was dark waters and thick clouds of the sky; and at another, that he dwelleth in light inaccessible and full of glory.

There are those who acknowledge the fact of a supernatural revelation, and yet determine beforehand what it must, what it *shall* contain. They come to the Bible, with a complete system of theology, morals, and even church government, elaborated in their own minds, not loosely sketched, but finished and rounded. The conclusion on all these grave subjects is fully resolved on, before the authoritative record is consulted. They then, with pertinacious diligence, hunt out whatever may be made to sustain their foregone conclusion; and with perverted ingenuity, distort or reject every thing against it. We can hardly say whether greater violence is done to human reason or to divine revelation, by such a procedure. An acknowledged revelation from God must partake of the supremacy which pertains to its author. What is the meaning, where is the use of a revelation, which is not to be *above* but *below* the authority accorded to the human mind? What intolerable arrogance in man to presume to sit in judgment on an accredited revelation from God, not to ascertain, but to determine its meaning! What a monstrous abuse of human reason! What an audacious affront to the divine majesty!

The design of God in revelation can be known infallibly and only from what the Scriptures actually contain. What then, in brief, do they principally teach? They teach explicitly and authoritatively, what man is to believe concerning God, and what duty God requires of man. The result of all speculative wisdom, the sum of all practical religion—in a word, the whole duty of man, is to fear God and keep his commandments. Correct apprehensions of the nature, the authority, and the contents of divine revelation, lie at the foundation of the piety which God approves; for the piety which God approves consists in right views of God, in right affections towards him, and in a correspondent course of action.

It is a remarkable fact, that the bitterest controversies, which have vexed the church of God, have turned upon matters, indeterminate, uncertain, and incapable of scriptural adjustment. There the Bible stands, immutably, inflexibly one, and the same amid the wars and changes of human opinion;

meanwhile, the fashions of this world passing away, revolutions perpetually taking place in systems of human philosophy, in theories touching the origin and destiny of man, in speculations concerning the origin and destiny of the earth which he inhabits; controversies in relation to the constitution, the character and the inhabitants of other, and often very distant bodies of the material universe, Geology, Astronomy, Metaphysics, Morals, Politics, all the waves of pedant pride and popular tumult, rising, raging, breaking against this our spiritual Gibraltar harmlessly; then retiring, their fury spent, to be succeeded by other systems of speculation, alike aggressive and alike impotent.

Unchangeableness, which is so essential an attribute of the Father of lights, is one of the most marked characters of that marvellous book, which unfolds to man His eternal counsels. Schools of philosophy, systems of science, methods of interpretation, spring up; live through their appointed day; die, and are heard of no more. But the Bible, although often misinterpreted, distrusted, corrupted, and opposed, is self-consistent, indestructible, and invariably triumphant. It is a thing well-worthy of being pondered, that those very sciences, which in their infancy seemed irreconcilably at variance with this blessed book, in their maturity have borne witness to the more than mortal wisdom of the holy men, who were moved to write it, and as willing captives have joined themselves to its chariot-wheels to swell its triumphs and to sound its praise! It becomes the friends of God then to honour his holy word by a calm, unfaltering trust; neither torturing its language into a forced conformity with the supposed testimony of infant sciences, nor rejecting the clear demonstrations of science, from the foolish fear that they will be found to clash with the recorded revelations of God.

No one need dread, lest the testimony of the rocks or of the stars, when read aright, should be at variance with the testimony of the Bible, rightly interpreted. "Hath the rain a father? or who hath begotten the drops of dew? Out of whose womb came the ice? and the hoary frost of heaven who hath gendered it? Canst thou bind the sweet influences of Pleiades, or loose the bands of Orion? Canst thou bring forth Mazzaroth in his season? or canst thou guide Arcturus with his sons? Knowest thou the ordinances of heaven? Canst thou set the dominion thereof in the earth?" Job xxxviii. 28—33.

What would now remain of the primitive revelation of God, if it had been adjusted to every change in science, to every phase in philosophy, to every transient doctrine in morals, to every imaginary improvement of the times—if it had been left in the hands of men to be twisted, dropped, squared, stretched, according to their will? Not a shred! not a fragment! It is likewise a truth, well worthy of remark, that some of the bitterest controversies have turned not upon the *fact*, or the *necessity*, or the *result* of God's supernatural operation, but upon the *mode* of the divine working. Now it is highly important to bear in mind, that the latter strictly belongs to Him, of which it may be we can have no knowledge, while the former may be of the number of our most sacred beliefs and duties. Thus in regard both to the material and to the spiritual creations. I may be wholly ignorant or incurious concerning the *method* of the creation, the worker in the process, and even in the period employed in calling into existence, and arranging in their relative forms and orders, the various tribes and species of his diversified creation, from the lowest to the highest. I may believe with Dr. Chalmers, that an indefinite period intervened between the original act of creation referred to in the first two and a half verses of Genesis, and the cosmical arrangement detailed in the succeeding verses of the first and second chapters. I may believe with Dr. Pye Smith, that the chaos of darkness and confusion was of limited extent. I may hold with Hugh Miller, that the days of Genesis first, were not natural days, as Dr. Chalmers and Dr. Pye Smith believed, but vast periods of indefinite duration; or I may never have thought or heard of the matter at all; and all or either, in perfect consistency with the deepest reverence for the Scriptures, as divinely inspired and divinely binding alike on faith and reason. For each of these illustrious men believed as fully in the divine origin and authority of the Mosaic record, as the simplest Christian in all the world. There are many things in regard *to the mode* of the creation, in respect to which intelligent believers may innocently differ; but in regard to *the fact*, there can be no difference of sentiment, because he who denies it, not only ceases to be, in any sense, a Christian, but proclaims himself an Atheist.

So in regard to the new creation of the soul in the spiritual image of its Maker. There are many things in relation to the work of the Spirit, in enlightening, attracting, subduing, sanctifying, and comforting the believer, which we cannot explain. But the fact, that rational and credible persons have been the conscious subjects of such a supernatural change, we can no more doubt than we can doubt our own existence. It is not only affirmed by innumerable and most trust-worthy persons of themselves as the conscious subjects of a spiritual renovation, in their desires, purposes, tendencies, hopes, and fears, but it is the promise of God to as many as should receive his Son, that they should have power to become the sons of God ; " which were born not of blood, nor of the will of the flesh, nor of the will of man but of God." Still, while the fact is clearly affirmed both of God and man, the *mode* of the Spirit's operation is confessed of one and authoritatively declared of the other, to be obscure and inscrutable. While the one gives, as the sum of his witness, this testimony, "I know that whereas I was blind, now I see;" the other says, "The wind bloweth where it listeth, and thou hearest the sound thereof, but canst not tell whence it cometh, and whither it goeth; so is every one that is born of the Spirit." John iii. 8. "For what man knoweth the things of a man, save the spirit of man which is in him? Even so the things of God knoweth no man but the Spirit of God. For who hath known the mind of the Lord, that he might instruct him?" 1 Cor. ii. 11–16.

The obvious design of God, in giving us a supernatural revelation, was to furnish certain intelligence on the most important truths. Those matters therefore, which it is most essential that we should know, are most clearly revealed.

> The primal duties shine aloft like stars;
> The charities that soothe and heal and bless
> Are scattered at the feet of man like flowers;
> The generous inclination, the just rule,
> Kind wishes and good actions and pure thoughts:
> No mystery is here.

If a man were giving a chart to his fellowman, travelling for the first time through an unknown country, he would naturally set down, most plainly, the largest objects, the highest mountains, the principal rivers, the widest expanse of lake and moor: and if any two intelligent persons should examine such a chart together, and a dispute arise concerning the way-marks, we might expect it to turn upon the less considerable objects, which had been wholly overlooked or obscurely indicated. Now the Bible is an inspired chart of the way of life: and shall God be reckoned less wise or less compassionate in its construction, than a man would be? They who hold the grand and cardinal doctrines of the Christian revelation, and whose lives accord with them, have the same precious inheritance; and should rejoice together as equally partakers of the common salvation. There ought then to be no fierce controversies among men, who agree in holding what both concede to be fundamental truth.

It is a nearly related consideration and of the same peace-making tendency, that the further we recede from the obvious teachings of Scripture by rational deduction, the more uncertain our conclusion, and the less likely to commend itself to the reason and conscience of another. Many men contend for the dark and doubtful inferences from a long and intricate chain of reasoning, with not less vehemence, than for the first principles of the doctrine of Christ; and represent them as not less binding on the faith of Christians generally. Nothing can be more unjust and unreasonable. The further we depart from what is plainly laid down in Scripture, the less authoritative and the less binding our conclusion.

We are prone to resent the restraints which divine revelation lays upon our reason and our will; but the greatest curse which God, in pitiless wrath, could inflict upon us, would not be to annihilate us at once and for ever; but to let us live on for ever and leave us without any authoritative rule of conduct or definition of duty, to put out the light of truth, to take away the key of knowledge, to deny the consolations of grace, and extinguish the hope of glory.

LECTURE VI.

APPARENT DISCREPANCIES TOUCHING JUSTIFICATION.

WHEN we look at any point of the visible horizon, it is but a very small portion of that glorious circle which we can embrace at a glance. Turning our eyes in one direction, we necessarily turn our backs upon the opposite point of the compass. If we had the hundred eyes of the fabled Argus—eyes before and behind and on either side—if, in a word, the whole body were one seeing faculty, we might survey the whole circle of the heavens at once.

Precisely so is it with us in regard to moral truth; we cannot take it in at once, in all its bearings and in all its beauty; in the act of looking at one truth we turn our backs on another at the opposite pole. This arises, evidently, not from any want of clearness or of prominence in the truth itself, but from the infirmity of our faculties. God alone can take in at a glance the boundless and beautiful circle of universal truth. To him—the infinite and essential Light—the Father of lights and Fountain of light—no part of that circle is in shadow—no part is unseen. His eye rests at the same moment on all the propositions which constitute the sum of universal truth.

What may be justly predicated of other truth, that it is consistent with itself, may, with the utmost confidence, be claimed for inspired truth. Sometimes this harmony may not be apparent, and then it becomes a matter of faith. Sometimes it is obscured by difficulties, which arise from our ignorance, and which disappear before fuller knowledge; but of this fact we may rest assured, that there is no real contradiction in inspired truth—that it is all capable of harmonious adjustment—that those truths which to us seem most mysterious and remote, pursue their even course, like the mighty and marshalled hosts of heaven, which, though separated by vast spaces and altogether invisible to mortal eyes—yet march on in beauteous order to the eye of God, and make sweetest melody in the Creator's ear.

The testimony of the Apostles Paul and James touching the matter of justification, furnish the most remarkable instance, perhaps, in all the Bible of an apparent contradiction.

Paul says expressly that we are justified by faith alone, without works. Gal. ii. 16; Rom. iv. 1–4. James says, in terms equally express, we are not justified by faith without works, but that we are justified by works also. James ii. 21–24. And as an illustration of his doctrine, each appeals to the case of Abraham. Thus at first sight, there seems to be a palpable contradiction throughout. So hopeless and invincible did the difficulty seem to Luther, that at one time he rejected the epistle of James from the Sacred Canon, and stigmatized it as an epistle of straw. He afterwards, however, corrected his judgment concerning the canonical authority of this epistle, as subsequent editions of the German Bible testify.*

*Turrettin's Theology, vol. 4. Special dissertation De Concordia Pauli et Jacobi in Articulo Justificationis. The method of reconciling these two apostles adopted by Turrettin in his acute and learned discussion, and by Owen in his massive and masterly treatise on Justification, had not escaped the penetration of Augustine, the profoundest theologian among the Latin fathers. In his commentary on psalm xxxi., he thus remarks: Jam qui audit, non ex operibus, sed ex fide, observet illam voraginem, de qua locutus sum: Vides ergo quia ex fide, non ex operibus justificatus est Abraham; faciam ergo quidquid volo, quia etsi bona opera non habuero, et tantum credidero in Deum, deputatur mihi ad justitiam. Si dixit et decrevit, lapsus demersus est; si adhuc cogitat et fluctuat, periclitatur. Scriptura autem Dei verusque intellectus, non solum periclitantem a periculo liberat, sed et demersum a profundo elevat. Respondeo ergo tanquam contra Apostolum et dico de ipso Abraham quod invenimus etiam in Epistola alterius apostoli, qui volebat corrigere homines, qui male intellexerant istum apostolum. Jacobus enim in Epistola sua, contra eos qui volebant bene operari de sola fide praesumentes, ipsius Abrahae opera commendavit, cujus Paulus fidem; et non sunt sibi adversi Apostoli. Dicit autem opus omnibus notum, Abraham filium suum immolandum Deo obtulit (Jacobi ii. 21) magnum opus, sed ex fide.

In the rejection of this epistle he was followed by the Magdeburg Centuriators. The Epistle of James was one of the last portions of Holy Writ to be received into the Sacred Canon; not so much from any deficiency of external evidence, as because it was thought that this Apostle's doctrine concerning the efficacy of works, was in direct conflict with the scriptural doctrine of justification by faith in Christ, without the works of the law. This, together with the final and general reception of the Epistle into the Sacred Canon, proves, first, that the difficulty was great enough to be felt by the church; secondly, that still it was not invincible.

I now proceed to show that there is no real discrepancy in the apostolic testimony, however real and great it may at first appear. Two knights of yore are said to have quarrelled about the inscription on a shield, and afterwards found that they were both right; for they had been looking at the same shield, but from different sides. So it is in regard to the matter in hand. There was no real contradiction between the knights, and there is none between the Apostles. What each knight said of his side of the shield was true, and what each of these Apostles says of justification and faith is true. But the knights were not speaking of the same side of the shield, and the Apostles were not speaking with

Laudo superædificationem operis, sed video fidei fundamentum; laudo fructum boni operis, sed in fide agnosco radicem.

the same design, of the same justification, of the same faith, or of the same characters. The difference between them, therefore, is verbal and apparent only, not real and essential. This will be evident:

First, from a consideration of the design and scope of each. The free justification of the sinner before God, by faith alone, is the ruling thought of Paul's mind, and the reigning thought of all his epistles and addresses. In its foundation, development, proofs, and consequences, it occupies the larger part of the Epistle to the Romans, by far the most extended and elaborate of his writings. It is prominently put forward in the Epistles to the Galatians and to the Ephesians, and is recognized and affirmed throughout his epistles generally. He was the chosen champion of the doctrine, which, according to the great Luther, is the article of a standing or of a falling church. Paul was the great Protestant of that day against the manifold corruptions and anti-evangelical errors of the Jewish Theology, errors which have their deep foundation in human nature; and have reappeared in various forms, and under different names in all subsequent ages. The student of the Scriptures and of church history, will continually find ancient errors and devices represented as the discoveries of modern science, and the fictions of yesterday proclaimed as the high, unquestioned truths of antiquity. Some historical acquaintance not only with the current belief of the Jews in

Paul's day, but of the circle of errors through which Greek philosophy ran, is necessary to a full understanding of the Apostle Paul; especially the first of his Epistles to the Corinthians and that to the Romans. Beginning with proud pretension, it ended in absolute and universal scepticism; professing to be able to explain all mysteries, or aspiring to do it, it ended with doubting all existence, all truth, all thought.* The errors against which Paul protested so vehemently are precisely those against which Augustine contended manfully in the fifth century; and Luther, Calvin, Zuingli, Knox, Cranmer, and other faithful reformers in the sixteenth. The root of all these errors was and is, that fallen man has in himself a recuperative energy, that he can do something effectual and meritorious, toward restoring himself to the favour and fellowship of God. It matters not, in regard to the deadly effect of this error, whether it rest on a denial of the total depravity and consequent helplessness of apostate man, or whether it proceed from some assumed relaxation of the holy rigour of the divine law, or upon a special covenant made

* It is remarked by G. H. Lewes in his History of Philosophy: Vol. ii. p. 136: that modern sceptics have added nothing, which is not implied in the principles of the Pyrrhonists. The arguments by which Hume thought he destroyed all the grounds of certitude, are differently stated from those of Pyrrho, but not differently founded; and they may be answered in the same way.

with a particular family or nation; it is, on either hypothesis and in any case, equally unscriptural, and altogether destructive of the grace of the gospel. The design of Paul, consistently carried out in all his extant addresses and epistles, was to correct the prevailing errors on this subject, and authoritatively expound the real method of justification before God. This he does by showing that all men, Jews and Gentiles, are alike sinners against a known law; that the sin is in every instance only aggravated in proportion to the clearness and fulness of the revelation; that the covenant made with Abraham was not designed to secure the salvation of all his natural descendants, without respect to their personal character; that the rite of circumcision was so far from conveying a justifying virtue that it was itself the seal of the righteousness of faith; that the blood of Jesus Christ afforded the only sacrifice for the sins of men; that his perfect obedience not only satisfied but magnified the law; and finally that through faith the justifying righteousness of Christ was imputed to the believer, so that he, for Christ's sake and for his sake alone, was discharged from the obligation to die and was received as righteous before God. The righteousness of Christ imputed to him, being the righteousness of God, manifest in the flesh, and the sufferings of Christ accepted for the expiation of his sins, being the agonies not of a mere man, nor of a mighty angel, but of one who was truly and in the most peculiar, exclusive, and exalted sense, the Son of God, the justified sinner, according to Paul's teaching, is not only free from all the penal demands of the law, which by his sins he had broken; but is brought nearer to God, and is more inseparably united to him than Adam was before the fall.

The relation which faith bears to salvation in the theology of Paul, is very distinctly marked and is of vital consequence. It does not justify, because it is itself meritorious or the ground of our salvation, for Paul assumes or asserts, throughout, that no creature can lay God under obligation or can properly be said to merit anything good; still further that no sinner can, while a sinner and as a sinner, do anything pleasing to God; still further that justifying faith is itself the gift of God, through Jesus Christ our Lord. What then, according to Paul, is the relation of faith to justification? It is, simply, that of an instrument by which we lay hold of and rest upon the strength and merit of another. Faith saves us, because by faith we receive Christ Jesus, the anointed and almighty Saviour, in his true character, in his proper office, as a gracious and God-given Redeemer from sin and death and hell. It is the link which unites the soul dead in sins to Christ, the source of spiritual and immortal life; and as the dead man revived when he touched the bones of the prophet, so the dead soul revives when brought into contact with the Lord of life. Faith has no virtue in itself, save as it puts us in connection with Him who is made unto us of God wisdom, righteousness, sanctification, and redemption. Faith saves us, because by faith we come to Christ, the Saviour. We receive him; we believe on him, and by his grace we are his and he is ours.

The design of the Apostle James was entirely different from that of the Apostle Paul. It was not to speak of the method of our justification in the sight of God at all, but of the evidence of our justification in the sight of men, such as could be submitted to the intelligent judgment of our fellow-creatures, and should be satisfactory to ourselves and others. There seems to have been men in that day, who believed and taught that the nominal renunciation of Paganism or Judaism, and the bare profession of the Christian faith, was enough to save them, while they retained all their ancient vices, or were at least total strangers to the purity, benevolence, and charity of the gospel. The manifest design of James was to rebuke their practical immoralities and neglects—to show that these were inconsistent with the Christian profession, at war with the benevolent spirit of the gospel, and incompatible with its most imperative obligations.

The faith of which Paul speaks as justifying, is not the faith which James affirms that it cannot justify. So far are they from being the same, that they have not one thing except the name in common. According to the uniform testimony of Paul, the faith which justifies a sinner before God, is never found alone. It is a faith which works by love and purifies the heart. It is variously and vitally connected with every other Christian grace, and it establishes its own identity; it proves and proclaims itself a divine faith, only when it is evidently productive and powerful, a root from which every other noble virtue springs, and of which heavenly charity is "the bright consummate flower." Hence, this very apostle thus exhorts his Philippian brethren: "Whatsoever things are true, whatsoever things are honest, whatsoever things are just, whatsoever things are pure, whatsoever things are lovely, whatsoever things are of good report, if there be any virtue, and if there be any praise, think on these things." Phil. iv. 8.

It is a very striking illustration of the apostles' harmony in doctrine, that Peter commences his glorious catalogue, his golden band of Christian virtues, with this radical and fruit-bearing grace. "And besides this, giving all diligence, add to your faith, virtue [or manly energy]; and to virtue knowledge; and to knowledge temperance; and to temperance patience; and to patience godliness; and to godliness brotherly kindness; and to brotherly kindness charity." 2 Peter i. 5—7.

Such is the faith connected with every Christian virtue, productive of every Christian grace, and flowering out in love; such is the faith that Paul says justifies without the works of the law. It justifies alone, but not being alone. The works, however, with which it is invariably found connected in our experience, are in no sense the cause, but in every case the effect and the evidence, of our justification before God.

Now let us compare, or rather contrast with this, what is predicated of the faith of which the Apostle James affirmed that it cannot justify. It is a faith, the very essence of which is profession or presumption. It is not found associated with other graces. It does not produce good works. It is not fruitful, but barren; not living, but dead; not saving, but worthless. It is not faith in deed, but in name only. It can deny a starving brother. It cannot clothe a naked sister. It is a faith no better than the faith of devils, who believe and tremble, but not adore and love; a faith seeming and spurious, not real and genuine—like bad money, which may have the name of the king upon it, but is made of base metal—copper for gold, and lead for silver. The faith then, of which the two apostles speak, is not the same faith. Paul is speaking of a living faith, whose fruits and proofs he gives. James of a dead faith, without works and every way worthless. Since, therefore, they do not speak of the same faith, there is no real contradiction between them.

The truth is, that the other apostles urge the indispensable necessity of good works, as the proper evidences of regeneration, quite as freely as James, when the occasion demands it. Thus Paul says of Christians, that they are "created in Christ Jesus unto good works." Eph. ii. 10. He says the design of Christ's death was "to purify to himself a peculiar people, zealous of good works." Titus ii. 14. He not only inculcates good works in general, but in numberless places urges the obligation of particular duties, and affirms that it is a distinctive mark of the gospel doctrine, that it is a doctrine according to godliness, and says of wicked men that while they profess to know God, yet in works they deny him. Titus i. 16. I have dwelt on these testimonies from Paul, the more fully, because it has been thought that his doctrine was diametrically opposed to the doctrine of James; and that while one was the champion of faith, the other was the champion of works. The Apostle John, besides urging particular duties, such as the forgiveness of offenders, and kindness to the poor, almost in the words of James, 1 John iii. 17, sums up all the evidences of love to God in one, keeping his commandments.

As the faith of which Paul speaks is different from that of which James speaks, so also is the justification. Paul intends justification in the sight of God. James intends justification in the sight of men. Paul refers to that "act of God's free grace wherein he pardoneth all our sins and accepteth us as righteous in his sight, only for the righteousness of Christ imputed to us and received by faith alone." Eph. i. 7; 2 Cor. v. 21; Rom. v. 19. James refers to the demonstration to ourselves and others, that we are justified persons—a demonstration which cannot be made or conceived of, except by works and through works. Paul's object is to exhibit the method by which a guilty sinner is pardoned and accepted of God, and obtains a clear title to the heavenly inheritance. The object of James is not to declare the method of justification before God, but to show wherein Christian character consisted and whereby it might be evinced. His sole and simple purpose is to show by what effects and arguments we may rightly conclude, who are justified persons.

Keeping in mind the facts, that the two apostles are speaking of a different faith, of a different justification, and of characters widely different: the one of a living and working, the other of a dead and worthless faith; the one of justification before God, the other of justification before men; the one of a conscious and convinced sinner, the other of a sensual and false-hearted Antinomian, we may now see how they might both appeal with equal propriety to Abraham as a practical illustration of the truth taught.

James says that Abraham was justified by works, and the particular work intended was the offering up of Isaac at the command of God. This, taken in all its circumstances, is the most illustrious act of obedience recorded of any mere man; and every word of that command seems purposely selected to heighten the trial and magnify the triumph of the patriarch's obedience. "And he said, Take now thy son, thine only son Isaac, whom thou lovest, and get thee into the land of Moriah, and offer him there for a burnt-offering upon one of the mountains which I will tell thee of." Gen. xxii. 2. Isaac was the son of his old age, the child of promise, the heir of the covenant, born by miracle, the progenitor of the Messiah. The act of obedience was not of such a nature that it could be instantly despatched, but was to be postponed as to its consummation for several days, and this dear son was to die, not by the common visitation of men, not by slow disease, not by sudden accident, not even by hostile violence at the hand of a stranger, but by an uplifted knife in his father's hand. We know how hard it is for a parent to bear the death of a beloved son, even when he falls in the path of glory and of duty. Oliver Cromwell tells us—strong-hearted soldier as he was—that the death of his son, slain in battle, went to his heart like a dagger. Edmund Burke soon followed to the grave the remains of his gifted son, whose genius he fondly believed superior to his own, and whose loss he did not wish to survive.*

*Nothing can be more affecting than the language in which Burke deplores the death of his son: "The storm has gone over me; and I lie like one of those old oaks which the late hurricane has scattered about me. I am stripped of all my honours; I am torn up by the roots and lie prostrate on the earth. I am alone, I have none to meet my enemies in the gate; desolate at home, stripped

Could anything be imagined, therefore, better adapted to show that the faith of Abraham was real, practical, supernatural? Could anything better illustrate the view of the nature, design, and office of faith, which the Apostle James had given, than this incident in the life of Abraham? Did not this heroic act of obedience prove him a justified person to himself, to his nation, to us, and to all men? Was not the plaudit of Jehovah just? "For now I know that thou fearest God, seeing thou hast not withheld thy son, thine only son, from me." Gen. xxii. 12.

Now let us see how reasonably and forcibly the case of Abraham is alleged by Paul, to illustrate his doctrine of the justification of a sinner before God, without works and by faith alone. This sublime act of obedience on the part of Abraham was not the cause of his justification, but the evidence and the fruit of it. For he was in a justified state at the very time of its performance, Moses and Paul being witnesses, and not only so, we have the same divine warrant for affirming that at the period of his offering up Isaac, he had been in a justified state for thirty years. In the fifteenth chapter of Genesis, referring to a period thirty years antecedent, it is said "he believed in the Lord, and he counted it to him for righteousness." Gen. xv. 6. Finally, it is said by the Apostle Paul, "And he received the

of my boast, my hope, my consolation, my helper, my counsellor, and my guide."—*Prior's Life of Burke.*

sign of circumcision, a seal of the righteousness of the faith, which he had yet being uncircumcised, that he might be the father of all them that believe, though they be not circumcised, that righteousness might be imputed to them also." Rom. iv. 11. So we may conclude assuredly, that there is no contradiction between those two apostles, but the most perfect accord since they speak respectively of a different faith—of a different justification—and of different characters.

If it be asked, Why this apparent discrepancy in the testimony of two inspired writers? we reply that it is designed to exercise our faith and stimulate our diligence. "What I do thou knowest not now, but thou shalt know hereafter," is the key to all the difficulties of Scripture. As there is the hiding of Jehovah's power, so there is the hiding of his purpose. When the difficulties are insoluble and insuperable, this concealment is to repress our intellectual pride and rebuke our rash judgments. "Canst thou by searching find out God? Canst thou find out the Almighty to perfection?" In the mind of God and in the counsels of God there is infinite harmony; but that harmony is not always evident to us. We may see that several propositions are contained in what we acknowledge to be a divine revelation; and yet we may not be able to perceive their consistency and correspondence. The proper course in that case is to take each on its own proper evidence, and wait for the fuller light of heaven to shine upon them and show their mutual accordance.

When, however, the difficulty is of such a nature that it may be removed or subdued by careful study, the plain design of providence in permitting it, is to stimulate our diligence in the investigation of truth. And this design is not more obvious than beneficent. Many a truth passes lightly over the surface of the mind because it is so evident and familiar; and many a passage of great preciousness and profound significance is slightly regarded because its import is obvious. It is an acute and characteristic observation of Coleridge that, "Truths of all others the most awful and interesting, are too often considered as so true, that they lose all the power of truth, and lie bed-ridden in the dormitory of the soul, side by side with the most despised and exploded errors." The very difficulties that we meet with in the study of the Scriptures, not only provoke inquiry but increase our strength and brighten our joy, when submitted to with humility or surmounted with success. Just as when a man is walking on level ground, he is apt to walk on lazily or turn aside lightly; but when he has to ascend a high and rugged hill, or wade through a deep and perilous morass, he gathers up his strength and girds himself for labour.

We have seen that Paul presents our justification in one of its aspects, and James in another; separate and distinct, but not in conflict or contradiction.

A corollary may be drawn from either aspect of the subject worthy of our consideration.

The first is the importance of keeping the law and the gospel strictly separate in the matter of our justification before God. This is not a secondary concern—a thing of speculation or theory, but of prime necessity, of supreme moment. It is not a matter in which our Christian comfort and clearness alone are involved, it is a matter of life and death with us. There is but one method of justification for a sinner before God, and that is the method revealed in the gospel by faith on the Lord Jesus Christ, a Saviour objectively presented, a Saviour out of ourselves, a Sacrifice of infinite merit and power. We cannot trust partly in him, and partly in ourselves, in our repentance, our faith, our reformation, our love, our humility, our prayers, our tears, our benefactions, or anything that is ours, either as wrought in us, or done by us. We may not divide the work or the glory with him. We must be content to receive a free pardon and hope in a gracious Saviour. Do this, and you need never fear falling into condemnation; he will receive you as you are, and make you what you ought to be; he will take you in the roughness and pollution of your nature, and make you a pure and polished pillar in the temple of our God whence you shall no more go out for ever. He will look upon you in your nakedness and blood, cast out as defiled and loathsome and execrable, and he will wash you in clean water and clothe you in a shining robe, and put a ring on your hands and shoes on your feet. His salvation is of pure grace. He came not to call the righteous but sinners to repentance: Christ is God's free gift: the Spirit is his free gift: heaven is his free gift: repentance, faith, perseverance, and eternal glory—all that accompanies, accomplishes, and constitutes salvation, all is his free gift.

The second is the importance of guarding against practical Antinomianism, or the profane notion, that we believe in Christ, we are orthodox Christians, and, therefore, we shall be saved, though we live not as becometh the gospel. The great danger with many in our time, is a forgetfulness of James' doctrine, that we are justified by works also, and not by faith alone, that our faith itself is justified, and our Christian confession can be justified only by works. Already we can discern clear signs of impatience in many, when the binding obligation of good works is urgently exhibited. Such teaching is stigmatized as legal teaching. If this is legal teaching, then Paul was a legal teacher, when he exhorted to "maintain good works for necessary uses." Tit. iii 14. And James, when he said, "Show me thy faith without thy works, and I will show thee my faith by my works." James ii. 18. And Peter, when he said, "As obedient children, not fashioning yourselves according to the former lusts in your ignorance: but as He which hath called you is holy, so be ye holy in all manner of conversation; because it is written, Be ye holy for I am holy." 1 Peter i. 14–16. And John, "Beloved, follow not that which is evil, but that which is good. He that doeth good is of God; but he that doeth evil hath not seen God." John iii. 11. And our Lord himself: "A good tree cannot bring forth evil fruit, neither can a corrupt tree bring forth good fruit. Every tree that bringeth not forth good fruit is hewn down, and cast into the fire. Wherefore by their fruits ye shall know them." Matt. vii. 18–20. In the dispensation of God, our sanctification flows from our justification, but in the experience of man, we infer our justification from the consciousness of our sanctification. The only certain evidence, therefore, which a man can exhibit to satisfy himself or another that he has faith, is afforded by his works. Mere profession without works is mere delusion, or presumption, or hypocrisy. The pretence of piety without the mortification of sin, without justice, truth, conscientiousness, humility, self-denial, alms-giving, brotherly-kindness, and charity is inexpressibly odious in the sight of God, our Supreme Judge, injurious to the souls of our fellowmen, and a high aggravation of every other sin.

LECTURE VII.

THE CHRISTIAN RELIGION, THE LEAVEN OF LIFE.

How different the emotions which the spectacle of Athens awakened in the souls of Cicero and of Paul! both of whom saw this illustrious city, as we know, and at no great interval of time. The one surveyed it with the eye and the heart of a heathen; although a philosopher, a scholar, a statesman, and an orator. He instinctively and delightedly recalled its ancient glories; the voices of the gifted dead still rang in his ears; the awful tones of Demosthenes aroused a sympathetic dread or an admiring glow, in the heart of the orator. The splendid rule of Pericles spoke to the statesman; those structures, which even in decay and in fragments, have been the admiration and despair of succeeding ages, appealed to his sense of the beautiful, still more deeply touched by the unrivalled productions of the pencil and the chisel, fit ornaments of such architecture; and then, as the crown of all, the intellectual glories, which like a spiritual halo encircled those wondrous works of art, those matchless

12 *

triumphs of the painter, the sculptor, and the architect—temples and theatres, which revived the hoar majesty of Æschylus, the moral wisdom and pathetic vehemence of Euripides, the artistic skill, the harmonious grandeur, and the consummate grace of Sophocles.

The actual emotions excited in the mind of the apostle are not left to conjecture. His spirit was stirred within him, when he saw the city wholly given to idolatry. He seems not to have had an eye or a thought for inferior interests, although no stranger to the culture of the Greeks. What to him were the graceful proportions of the Parthenon, or the glories of the famous Pnyx, where the greatest of orators had so often held spell-bound the most imaginative and the most impulsive souls to whom human eloquence had ever been addressed? What to him were the artistic triumphs of Phidias or Praxiteles, when the orator in the height of his great argument, though a Pericles or a Demosthenes, could appeal only to an unknown God? and what to him were the æsthetic attractions of a temple or image, if that temple were dedicated to Minerva or to Venus, and that image consecrated to Jupiter or Mars? He felt that men's religious interests were their highest interests, that God's best gift to man was the gospel, though foolishness to the Greek; that it was the most potent factor and the most precious element that had ever entered into the history and heart of man; that it was the tree of life, whose leaves were for the healing of the nations.

Men there are in the world who are not of the world, the good seed of the kingdom, children of the light and the day. The superficial may be able to discern no difference between them and others. There is nothing peculiar in their dialect, dress, diet, or occupation; but their principles, aims, instincts, spirit, their pains and pleasures, hopes, and fears, all are different from those of this world's children, their character in time and their destiny for ever! God the Creator and Father of all men, but by a double and a dearer title, their God and Father, does not regard them as he regards others. They are especially dear to him, his elect lot, his beloved heritage, his desired portion, "a garden enclosed, a spring shut up, a fountain sealed." Song iv. 12. For them he moves, controls, exalts, abases, all other agents; for them he orders all events and determines all their issues.

Accordingly, one thing especially remarkable about the Christian religion is the absolute identity of its manifestations all over the world and in all ages of the world; not merely the internal bond, that constitutes its essential unity, the conclusive fact that all its doctrines cohere and correspond, that there should be no irreconcilable conflict between statements of innumerable men of various nations, ranks, lineage, education, calling, and extending over a vast period of not less than sixteen centuries, from the author of the book of Genesis to the author of the book of Revelation; not this merely, but the practical spirit which it has evinced, and the practical fruits which it has borne in every soil and under every sky. In the four quarters of the globe, the faithful servants of the true God have been distinguishable, from the giving of the law on Mount Sinai to the preaching of the gospel on the Mount of Blessing; from the first century of the Christian era to the present day, by the same attributes, evincing the same traits, doing the same deeds, preferring duty to interest, rendering good for evil, and renouncing life rather than a good conscience.

Under every dispensation, the grand design of every revelation of grace has been to bring many sons unto glory; to redeem immortal souls from the deadly evils of the first apostasy, and conduct them to the full fruition of heavenly bliss. When one of our race is regenerated by the Holy Ghost, adopted into the family of God, and made an heir of eternal glory, Satan loses a slave and a victim, our Father in heaven gains a child and a worshipper for ever! What a change takes place in the spirit, the character, the destiny of the subject of that gracious adoption in time and throughout eternal ages! What wonder that the angels in heaven rejoice over a repenting sinner; that the Father of all rejoices; that the Son of God rejoices over the returning prodigal! If any man sin and one convert him, "let him know that he which convereth the sinner from the error of his way shall save a soul from death and shall hide a multitude of sins." James v. 20. Is it not worth then all the anxieties which the christian can endure, all the efforts that he can make, all the intercessions that he can employ, and all the indignities that he can suffer, to achieve such an end ?

The sovereign good of human nature is holiness, inward purity, consecration to God, in which alone we attain that freedom, dignity, and happiness, in which the proper perfection of our nature consists. This then is what all men should seek first and most; happiness will naturally follow in the wake of duty. Self-seeking is self-destruction. The direct pursuit of pleasure is the certain death of happiness. Nothing indeed should be mainly and primarily sought but duty. When a man has any other guide, seeks any other end, he is self-condemned; and the voice of his own condemning conscience is but the echo of the more awful voice of God. To fit us for heaven we need an inherent and subjective qualification, and this qualification is holiness, the washing of regeneration, and the renewing of the Holy Ghost. Heaven is an unmerited but not an arbitrary gift, and therefore not irrespective of moral fitness. Rev. xxi. 27. Without personal godliness, the perpetual presence of God would be the most abhorred thraldom, the most terrible woe.

Our preparation for heaven is a progressive work,

and God detains us upon the earth only till it is completed. We should indeed be saved if we were to die the moment the Saviour says, "Thy sins are forgiven thee;" but we have not a proper and perfect fitness for our purchased crown, until our work on earth is ended, the battle fought and the victory won. Addressing myself especially to young men, just entering on a religious course, I say, Press on, strive to enter in at the strait gate, remember that a crown, a kingdom is before you, a crown of righteousness and the kingdom of heaven. If a Christian at all, you will endeavour to be a growing Christian, and you will be. Until the end of your life you will be making daily progress in knowledge, zeal, love, devotion. You will have an increasing power in prayer, more courage and heart for duty. You will be more conscientious as you become more confirmed in holiness and wisdom. The painter with every touch of his brush gives more distinctness, delicacy, harmony, finish to his picture. Day by day, the sun and air cause a deeper shade to descend on the golden rind of the summer fruit, and add more sweetness to its luscious juices. So with Christian character, every day will add a finer tint, a livelier hue. Daily will evil passions be more perfectly subdued, faults confessed and corrected, errors detected and amended, under the discipline of Providence, the means of grace, and the teaching of the Holy Ghost.

The gospel is the great instrument of spiritual

regeneration, according to the commission of our Lord to the apostles, "Go ye into all the world and preach the gospel to every creature, teaching them to observe all things whatsoever I have commanded you, and lo! I am with you always, even unto the end of the world." Here we have the original affirmation of the teaching office of the church; the permanent commission of representatives and ministers, in its Author and purpose, in its terms and promise.

The whole world, then, is to be sought, to be reached, to be renovated. Unregenerate humanity is the corrupt mass; the gospel of the grace of God is the leaven which is to pervade and purify it. The church of the living God, small and unnoticed in its earlier progress and incipient movements, is destined when grown, to fill the earth with its fragrance and its fruit, as the grain of mustard seed which a man took and sowed in his field, "which indeed is the least of all seeds, but when it is grown is the greatest among herbs, and becometh a tree, so that the birds of the air come and lodge in the branches thereof." Matt. xiii. 32.

These characteristic images are supposed to set forth, with admirable aptness and completeness, the two-fold aspect and operation of the gospel, intensive and extensive, on the thoughts, affections, discourse, and conduct of the individual man, as they are progressively pervaded and transformed thereby; and its external operation on the forms and forces, the institutions and usages, the objects and interests of organized society.

The universal spread of the blessed gospel in its doctrine and spirit, in its power and glory, is the heaven-ordained process by which men are to be delivered from corruption, translated into a kingdom, and invested with a character of righteousness. To act upon this great truth is the office of faith; to put our trust in no earthly organization, in no human contrivance, in no system of man's device, in no scheme of philanthropy, in no scheme of benevolence; but in the pure and simple gospel, wherein is the wisdom of God and the power of God unto salvation. Honour the gospel, honour God, and he will honour you. Cast contempt upon him, his truth, his church, which is the pillar and ground of the truth, his chosen instrument to reform and save men, and he will overwhelm you and your presumptuous schemes with merited confusion and shame. Moral and benevolent societies are very good things, when directed to proper objects and under wise control; but they are not the gospel, and they are not the church. They never can be the instrument of the world's regeneration. All such pretensions are vain and fallacious, arrogant and wicked.

God's providence appears in so ordering all things—the minutest, the most painful, seemingly the most adverse and injurious—as to facilitate the conversion and effect the final salvation of his own people. His natural and gracious sovereignty over all elements, agents, events, and effects, in endless succession, is gloriously exercised in doing just what is needful; sending trouble when, where, in the form, in the way, and in the measure, in which it will be most efficacious; at the same time operating within by his Spirit, on the thoughts and affections of the heart, so as most effectually to incline it to himself, and bind it fast in chains of heavenly love. Of one thing we have the absolute assurance, that Christ, as King, shall ultimately subdue, by his word and Spirit, all his and our enemies; among whom the chief and worst are unbelief, pride, rebellion, sinful anger, lust, superstition, covetousness, and the love of this present evil world.

Every man contributes to the diffusion of the gospel, as himself imbued with its spirit and power. As himself leavened, he is not only one taken from the corrupt mass, and so in an individual and isolated form leavened; but he directly spreads the hallowed influence, and so the saving process goes on, until a family, a state, a nation, a world is leavened. The man, who is not faithful to every other man's soul, is not faithful to his own. The man who does not properly care for, pray for, and labour for the conversion and edification of every member of his family, of every human being in the proportion of his personal claims on his Christian charity, is not faithful to his own spiritual interests.

So wisely hath God identified our own comfort and safety, with the punctual discharge of our duty to the souls of all others; and so effectually hath he provided for the universal diffusion of gospel light and truth!

Men do not stand apart, insulated, alone in this world. There is therefore in the saving conversion to God of a particular person, not the mere leavening of that one, not the subtraction of a single unit from the side of sin and Satan, and the carrying over of that single unit to the side of holiness and of the Saviour; there is not merely the kindling of one other light in a dark place, but there is the lifting aloft of one who shall shine, and cheer, and guide, by his own solitary radiance, but the putting into being and brightness one from whose blazing body innumerable other lights may be kindled in all lands and through all time. It is not the mere electrifying of a single substance, cut off from all communication with every other, but it is the communication of the electric current to a whole battery at once, or in scarcely appreciable succession. The history of the propagation of religion in this way, from man to man, like men riding post and taking the truth from one point to another, from one person to another, like the fiery cross of Scotish story, the gleaming light borne far over hill and dale, by the first messenger committed to a second, who repeats the same process, and then he in turn gives it to a third, until the whole country is illuminated and aroused; or like men joining hands, in long succession and in a vast circle—such a history would be replete alike with interest and instruction. Thus from Adam to Enoch, from Enoch to Noah, from Noah to Abraham, from Abraham to David, and from David to Christ ; then taking the advent of the Redeemer as the second great starting-point, tracing this line of light over the vast spaces which have intervened ; some of them centuries of darkness, degradation, superstition, and shame ; but that line of light, though flickering and feeble, never quite extinguished, but still visible, and sometimes rising and beaming far and high with heavenly radiance, from Christ to Paul, from Paul to Augustine, from Augustine to Luther, from Luther to the present hour ! How strict and clear the connection between the conversion of many of these, as of Paul and Stephen, Augustine and Ambrose—Augustine from whose heaven-filled urn so many of God's faithful servants replenished their waning lamps, during the long night of Papal domination and darkness, till the rise of Martin Luther aud John Calvin, both of whom reverenced him as they reverenced no other uninspired mortal ; and in later days from William Wilberforce to Legh Richmond, from Legh Richmond to John Newton, and from John Newton to Thomas Scott.

Think of the leavening influence going out from all of these men ; from the great Protestant reformers of Germany, France, Switzerland, England, and

Scotland, personally by their preaching and example while they lived; by their writings and their prayers, which in different ways, have operated on the minds and hearts of men, since they died; and which must continue to live and work and spread,

"Till the last syllable of recorded time,"

"like a circle in the water, which never ceaseth to enlarge itself." The man who in any way contributes to the diffusion of this leaven by his life, his labours, his teaching, his prayers, or his money, is doing a certain, an endless, an incalculable good.

The better and nobler order of spirits have a high sense of intellectual obligation. They feel a strong personal attachment to their teachers, those who have led them into the secret chambers of moral wisdom, at first of difficult access it may be, but once entered, shining with a serene and heavenly light, garnished with pure gold and pearls and precious stones, and compassed about with goodly pillars and strong and stately walls. They feel a sentiment of personal gratitude to those who first elicited their dormant energies, furthered the development of their conscious powers, communicated to their minds a pleasure higher far than the wealth of Xerxes could purchase, or the banquets of Apicius afford—the pleasure that springs up in the soul on the perception of a new truth, or of an old truth in new forms, under new aspects, in new relations. Every scholar is sensible of a feeling akin to personal attachment to the great intellectual benefactors of the race, stars of the first magnitude in the firmament of letters; to Bacon "the minister and interpreter of nature," who so justly says of himself, "I have taken all knowledge to be my province;" to Milton, to whom it was given "to celebrate in glorious and lofty hymns the throne and equipage of God's almightiness, and what he works, and what he suffers to be wrought with high providence in his church; to sing victorious agonies of martyrs and saints, the deeds and triumphs of just and pious nations;" to Shakspeare "so noble in reason! so infinite in faculties!" How much greater, how much more worthy of grateful remembrance, obligations purely spiritual and religious! What do we not owe to the great Protestant Reformers, to our own spiritual pastors, who in labour and weariness, with many tears and temptations, have watched for our souls as they that must give account! Hereafter, how vain and empty will many objects seem, which now so engross and ensnare us! How lighter than the small dust of the balance, the aims of vulgar ambition, the petty gains and honours, the jealousies, the triumphs, the hopes and fears, which now so absorb and agitate us! When once the line that separates for us time and eternity has been passed, our brief and unreturning probation ended; of what infinite importance will purely spiritual labours and attainments seem!

All lands and times are bound together by thousand-fold influences. The aggregate of all history, known and unknown, the former chiefly affects the thinker—moulds the mind and heart of successive generations. We act on the future, and we in turn are acted on by the past. Every event in time, every thought of man, expressed in speech or action, is at once a seed and segment of universal history. It is this which throws such an immense responsibility around human opinion, feeling, and action. We cannot even in thought touch the utmost limit to which influence extends, or the innumerable avenues through which it goes forth. The knowledge of the influence which good and bad men respectively exert, is concealed from them in great part till eternity. God alone, who has given men their faculties and assigned their duties, to whom the ultimate and most awful responsibility is due, can fully estimate the infinite importance of faithful obedience to his own laws. Thus our very ignorance of the remote and possible consequences of our conduct should instruct us. Of whatever else we may be ignorant, we know that,

"Duty, stern daughter of the voice of God,"

is a sacred thing. We cannot tell how far the consequences of obedience or rebellion may reach, or how long they may endure. It is not our part to reckon consequences, or balance probabilities, but to obey laws. Who can estimate the remote issue of one act of resolute virtue or of one life of heroic service, like that of Moses or Paul, of Luther or Martyn?

The most potent agencies of nature are always slow and silent. When Jehovah spoke of old to the prophet, it was not in the great and strong wind which rent the mountains, nor in the earthquake, nor yet in the fire; but in the still, small voice; 1 Kings xix. 9–13; and so it has ever been. The wisest of us are very incompetent judges of the elevation and dignity, the magnitude or the extent, of moral forces. The kingdom of God cometh not with observation. Religion is making progress when the world, when the church, and the teachers and rulers of the church, are not dreaming of it. If we had "senses exercised to discern both good and evil;" Heb. v. 14; a more delicate tact wherewith to perceive spiritual things, the scarcely audible whisper of a divine truth as of the gentle sigh of the summer wind, passing over the tender grass, the scarcely formed footprints of the King of kings, as in noiseless majesty he passes by, the ethereal aroma of the Saviour's presence and working, so "that though he would not be known, yet he could not be hid," the obscure intimation of the glorious day in the first faint flush of the rising dawn, we should oftentimes be thankful and glad, when now we are cast down with sorrow and fear. It may serve, too, to show how shallow as well as audacious, are the flings and jeers of free-thinkers and pseudo-philosophers, like the Pantheist Carlyle, when they would fain have it believed that the Christianity of our time is worn out and worthless, incapable of heroic struggles and sacrifices, of the crown of martyrdom and the palm of victory.

Patient progress is the law of the kingdom of God on earth. Men are impatient and impulsive. They are for precipitating events, doing every thing at once, sowing the seed and reaping the harvest, the same day. Not so God, with whom a thousand years are as one day, and one day as a thousand years. The world was created successively, not simultaneously, all its kingdoms and species and races at once. Four thousand years were suffered to elapse from the apostasy to the redemption, from the expulsion of the first Adam from Eden in shame and sorrow, to the opening of "the most ancient" heavens to receive the second Adam, the triumphant and ascending Saviour, the glorious Conqueror of the gloomy realm of sin and death, the gracious Revealer and Giver of Paradise regained, a world of perfect joy and love, a region of perpetual light and sunshine and peace.

The providence of God is the gradual evolution and accomplishment of a far-reaching plan. Every step contemplates something beyond, is conditioned by the past, and connected with the future. The same great law applies to the three great kingdoms of nature, of providence, and of grace; in each there is first the grain, then the ear, after that the full corn in the ear. "Excelsior" is the Christian's proper motto, as it is his constant aim. He is called continually to purer and loftier heights of holiness, until at last, every sin subdued, and every stain effaced, he is invited to come up higher, above the starry heights, beyond the crystal sphere, aloof from the region of storm and tempest, of sin and death, to mansions of peace and glory prepared in heaven for him. The life that we now live is an education for eternity; and on the proper exercise, and discipline, and consequent development of our powers on earth, may depend the largeness, the variety, and the comparative glory of our final attainments. This may possibly be true, and most probably is true, in regard to the redeemed at least, of our purely intellectual progress, especially in the knowledge of what is revealed, and in obedience at once to the law of conscience and to the love of truth. It holds certainly and absolutely of our moral and spiritual attainments. The talent which is now wisely laid out, will there be found to have multiplied exceedingly, and yet in proportion to our present diligence. So that at death, there will not only be an immediate, but a prospective and progressive reward for our present faithfulness in self-culture in the service of God. Every stroke that is designed to bring out the living image of perfect excellence, will go sounding on through the noiseless slumber of the tomb, through the dateless ages of eternity. Still, we must never forget, that religion does not consist in speculative knowledge, or in sentimental virtue, or in motiveless action, or in constitutional benevolence, or in an external course of good living based upon earthly principles and affections. It is a life, created and kindled by the breath of God, having its seat in the soul, and its proof and power in all manifestations within and without; conscious and sensible in the affections, principles, and conduct.

Constant progress is the law of the religious life of the individual believer. The reason why any "that did run well" fall away, is the fatal thought that they can fall back, with impunity, that they can stand still without danger. Under these delusions, instilled by Satan and fostered by the corrupting example of nominal believers, they remit their diligence, cease their watchfulness, lose their tenderness of conscience, dally with what they call little sins, have no longer any sense of freedom and joy in prayer; a yawning chasm, a dreadful and increasing distance, now separates their souls from God. They are tottering on the verge of a deep abyss; at length, they commit some overt act of transgression, gross and scandalous. Their spot is evidently not the spot of God's children; they stand revealed to their own eyes, and to the view of all men, self-convicted and foul apostates. What, let us ask, is the origin—what the secret history of these melancholy cases? What but the absurd and unscriptural notion that they might dismiss all zealous concern, when they thought their sins forgiven, their peace made, their salvation sure? These are the successive steps and stages of their downfall. First they grow presumptuous, then they become lukewarm, then they relapse into worldliness, formality, sloth, and death! There is no better test of true piety, than that it continues to the end, and grows to the last. The promise is to such, and to such only. The principle of piety, when genuine, is permanent and progressive. It is diffusive, like light; it is pervasive, like leaven. Accordingly, we are exhorted to grow in grace and in the knowledge of our Lord and Saviour Jesus Christ.

The whole man in his thoughts, feelings, speech, conduct, objects, and interests, is to be pervaded and purified by the gospel. A true faith works at once, equally, and in all directions; in its nature, it is impartial; in its sphere, universal. It spreads through the whole mass. Other images are employed in Scripture to indicate the same general truth. Sometimes the gospel is represented under the image of leaven, diffusing itself through all the faculties of the soul; sometimes as a principle of life, giving rise to a spontaneous and symmetrical development. A normal and healthy growth implies a uniform expansion, a proportioned increase. This, we see in the graceful flower, its stalk swelling, its verdant branches putting forth tender buds, which in their time unfold in "the bright consummate flower." Thus, true piety, like leaven, spreads its sanctifying and salutary forces through all the mind, through all the man. It induces a regular and harmonious development of all the graces of the Spirit. It spares no vice, however pleasing and prevalent, however deep-seated and constitutional. It will not do for the passionate man, after he becomes a Christian, to excuse his unchristian outbreaks on the ground that his is a constitutional infirmity, a besetting sin. The faithful commander doubly fortifies the weak point, and places his most trusty sentinel at the post most liable to surprise and assault. "Wherefore, seeing we are also compassed about with so great a cloud of witnesses, let us lay aside every weight, and the sin which doth so easily beset us, and let us run with patience the race that is set before us." Heb. xii. 1.

It is then not less the command of God, than the dictate of reason, to guard with special vigilance against our besetting sins. If our religion be not thus impartial, comprehensive, and harmonious, it is not genuine, scriptural, saving. A single leak neglected may sink a ship; and a single sin indulged may damn a soul. The earnest and elevated believer is perpetually surrounded by a sense of duty, by the conscious presence of God, like an all-embracing atmosphere.

All the events of life may be made conducive to this leavening process; health and sickness, wealth and poverty, shame and honour, life and death, every dispensation of Providence, and every emotion of the heart. "All things work together for good to them that love God, to them that are the called according to his purpose. All things are yours, and ye are Christ's, and Christ is God's." Even our very sins may instruct us, may be made the instruments under God of teaching us a truer and deeper self-knowledge, of breeding within us a purer and more perfect humility, of making us more distrustful of our own imagined strength and holiness, of leading us to put our trust more simply in the all-sufficing grace of the Lord Jesus. Let not those therefore, who have fallen into open sin, and so brought dread and darkness on their own souls, and scorn on the holy name by which they were called, fall into despair. Satan would drive you to despair, but Christ calls you to repentance. Your only hope is in the recovering, pardoning grace of your injured, but still forgiving Father. Let your instant, incessant, and only appeal be to his mercy in Christ. Zech. xii. 10; Hosea xiv. 4–7. "Let your eyes look upon me whom you have pierced," says our loving, bleeding Saviour, "and mourn for him as one mourneth for his only son, and be in bitterness for him as one that is in bitterness for his firstborn. Take with you words, and turn to the Lord; say unto him, Take away all iniquity and receive us graciously, so will we render the calves of our lips:" Then will he turn and say unto you, "I will heal their backsliding, I will love them freely, for mine anger is turned away from him. I will be as the dew unto Israel; he shall grow as the lily, and cast forth his roots as Lebanon. They that dwell under his shadow shall return; they shall revive as the corn, and grow as the vine; the scent thereof shall be as the wine of Lebanon."

As the thoughts, the dispositions, the habits, the spirit, and life of the individual are to be leavened by the gospel, so the beliefs, the literature, the laws, the maxims, the manners, the principles, and the polity of nations, of the race, are all to be leavened in like manner. And the process is indicated in the leaven. It is to be silent, gradual, insensible, communicated. It is to be a real leavening. It is to spread from man to man; from land to land. The race is indeed a unit—as the individual is one; as the family is one; as the nation is one. We are made of one blood. We are redeemed by one Saviour. We are sanctified by one Spirit. We have all one Father. We look forward with glad hearts to one heaven. One of the race influences each; each of the race influences all. The injury I do myself, does not, cannot terminate with me. The saying so common among young men, "No man's enemy but his own," is a solecism, an absurdity, an impossibility. The man who is his own enemy is the enemy of the whole human race, just so far. He defrauds all whom he might have served: he injures by his death all whom he might have benefitted by his life. And his bad example may be all the more extensive, the more infectious, and the more mischievous if it gain currency and colour from accidental association with certain amiable and pleasing qualities, which are often found in the self-indulgent voluptuary. Of whatsoever he may seek to persuade himself, however he may be regarded by others, he is a genuine Ishmael; his hand is against every man. There is a trembling, wide-spread sensibility in the soul of man. The blow that strikes one wounds all men through all time. This is true of wickedness and of wicked men; pre-eminently true is it of moral goodness and of good men. That is only a half truth then, which Shakspeare utters when he says,

> The evil that men do lives after them,
> The good is oft interred with their bones.

In the providence of God, on the principle of accountability, neither the evil nor the good will ever cease to live and act and spread; neither the good nor the evil is interred with our bones. Each is vital, eternal, on earth, and in other worlds. Our influence for good or evil is boundless in duration and degree. It is fraught with a perpetual life. It is essentially, infinitely, eternally reproductive.

> Powers depart;
> Possessions vanish and opinions change,
> And passions hold a fluctuating seat;
> But by the storms of circumstance unshaken,
> And subject neither to eclipse nor wave,
> Duty exists—immutably survive,
> For our support, the measures and the forms,

Which an abstract intelligence supplies,
Whose kingdom is, where time and space are not.

God calls us to take part in a great work, in a great warfare; the accomplishment of many an ancient and glorious prophecy; the application to ourselves and others of the gracious and saving atonement; the diffusion of the gospel and the conversion of the world. Will you hearken? Will you do it? Christ has done his part. His work is finished and accepted. The Spirit of grace, the purchase of the Son, and the promise of the Father is ready to do his part. Will you do yours? Will you be co-workers with God? Will you seek to win souls? Will you pray, labour, suffer sacrifice in this holy cause, for this grand object? The importance of human action cannot be exaggerated, cannot be expressed, and the corresponding importance of a sound judgment, of a thoughtful mind, above all, of a conscience enlightened and controlled by the truth and Spirit of God. It is awe-inspiring to reflect upon the permanence, still more the propagation, of influence. The universe is a vast whispering gallery, wherein the least and lowest accent of truth, of faith, of prayer, of love, is no sooner uttered than it is taken up and repeated and reverberated everywhere and for ever.

The sin of Adam as our natural and our federal head, was in several respects peculiar, both as imputed and as transmitted; but every man's sin spreads abroad and afar disease, corruption, wretchedness, and death, in his own immediate circle, first and worst; then, in ever-widening circles, till it reaches the last man and the last moment; then, surviving the dissolution of all material things, it "spreads undivided," "operates unspent," through the illimitable ages of eternity.

That is a sublime passage in which Christ is represented as mounted on a white horse, going forth conquering and to conquer. It is a truly delightful thing to anticipate the gradual spread of the kingdom, which is not of this world, till in successive waves of light it sweeps over and gladdens and glorifies all lands,

> "Till like a sea of glory,
> It spreads from pole to pole,"

till with its heavenly power it pervades all the thoughts, interests, duties, and enjoyments of men.

It is sin that embitters human hearts and human life. Every institution of society might remain unchanged, the elements rage with their accustomed fury, the ground abide under the curse as of old, and yet what a mighty, what an instant, what a happy change would take place, if the heart of every man were suddenly to be imbued with the regenerating and sanctifying grace of the gospel! How would a peace, deep, delicious, calm, and pure as the heavens, descend into the soul! What blessedness past all comprehension would at once drop as the rain and distil as the dew on hearts now "dry as summer dust!" What a beauty would be reflected back from the beaming and blissful spirit on the unconscious world around us! and how would heaven and earth unite in harmony and praise! The reason why the regeneration of the world, its restoration to God, is so long delayed, is that Christians, through whose willing agency this happy consummation is to be effected, acquiesce in its present character and state, and intercede, and strive, and sigh so little, for a better and a brighter dispensation.

Ultimately, we know all will be leavened, but now much remains to be done. Look at literature, laws, art, science, social life. How far are all these from the pure and heavenly spirit of the gospel! Suppose all these animated and informed with the grace and glory of the sacred Scriptures, how raised, how radiant would they be! how resplendent with a beauty akin to that which rested on the fresh, unfallen creation!

Unfaithful as the church has been, still it should not be forgotten, that much has been accomplished already by the leavening power of the gospel. There are two classes of men of entirely opposite character, and impelled by directly opposite motives, who are prone to underrate the actual results of religious agencies. The first is the humble and zealous Christian, dismayed at the wickedness which still abounds in all places, in all persons, and especially in himself; despondent because so much less has been even attempted than his ardent and eager benevolence can conceive of, and burns to see accomplished. The other is the smiling infidel, who can coldly and proudly point to the ignorance and vice yet remaining in Christian communities, in Christian men, and on the untrodden wastes of heathendom, and ask, Where is the promise of his coming, what the fruit of eighteen centuries of teaching and effort? * Where are the triumphs of the gospel, where its trophies and monuments? We answer, If you seek its monuments, look around you; compare even yourself with your bloody pagan ancestors, the laws, the institutions, the literature, the moral and social state of modern Europe and the United States, with any part of the world and any period of the world before the advent of our Lord.

Whatever tends to exalt the spiritual part of man, to give the interests of the soul and of eternity prominence and dignity, as contrasted with the fugitive interests of time and of the perishable body, tends to the real honour of human nature. Of all things it is most ennobling to sacrifice material to spiritual interests. Hence the pre-eminent grandeur of the missionary enterprise, looked at from the lowest ground of contemplation. The commission of our Lord to his apostles, in which alone the church proceeds in all her plans to evangelize the nations, comprehends the interests of all the world. We should, therefore, pray and labour for the speedy conversion of all nations, because the longer that

* Westminster Review, *et id omne genus.*

blessed consummation is deferred, the more generations will go down to the grave without the knowledge of the only Saviour. The same Christian spirit which impels a man to go as a missionary to foreign lands, should induce him to use every effort to instruct the ignorant, awaken the careless, reclaim the erring, and save the lost around him. Alas! that we should be so prone to defer service! When shall we learn to do the work of the day in its season, to embrace with prompt alacrity every opportunity of doing good to the perishing souls of our fellow-men?

The necessity in nature for the doctrines of grace, the ground in reason and philosophy for the evangelical doctrine of spiritual regeneration is made clear when we consider the pervasive and assimilating quality of the Christian faith. "Except a man be born again, he cannot see the kingdom of heaven," is the personal testimony of the Lord Jesus, and it is a conclusion which all human experience, so far as it can be ascertained from the historical record of the characters and tendencies of our fallen race, amply confirms. The efforts which individual men of the better order have made to root out the evil affections of their nature, and raise their souls above sordid and sensual desires, have been lamentably vain; even morality, in its outward form and garb, has never appeared among any pagan people. The character of the most cultivated nations of profane antiquity was notoriously stained with the most detestable vices. Their most admired authors record of themselves with utter unconsciousness of wrong, or with visible elation of spirit, what cannot now be read without a blush. Nothing but the grace of God is stronger than human corruption. All the maxims of men, all the exhortations of men, all the devices of men, are vain to sanctify the soul. Thy blood, eternal Saviour, alone cleanseth us from all sin! Let me then urge all who know that they are unregenerate sinners, to betake themselves without delay to the Lamb of God, that taketh away the sin of the world. Trust in his atoning blood for pardon and peace. Humbly and with all your hearts cry to God, for the gracious Spirit of his Son to sanctify and save you.

There is no more amiable and majestic aspect of the church of the living God, than that which she sustains in her ordained and historic relation to the missionary enterprise. It pertains to the very essence of piety in an individual or a community to be communicative, to diffuse itself. When Andrew had found the Saviour, he made haste to tell Peter, and he Nathanael. The faith of God, the love of Christ, is a fire in the bones. It cannot be suppressed; it cannot be concealed; it cannot be confined; it will discover itself; it will propagate itself. By its very charter, the church of the Lord Jesus Christ is a missionary institution. If it cease to make progress, it ceases to be fruitful, to be strong, to be pure. Like the pool of Bethesda, its waters must be agitated, to exert their healing virtue. Historically regarded, the purity and vigour of the church are nearly convertible terms. In the ages in which she has been most holy in doctrine, in life, and in spirit, she has made most extensive and glorious progress. Look at her during the apostolic period, magnificently endowed with truth and grace, majestic, free, full of inward and irrepressible life, going forth to the spiritual conquest of the world, with nothing but the Shepherd's sling and stone, but guided by Jehovah and girt about with his invincible strength, therefore "fair as the moon, clear as the sun, and terrible as an army with banners." The energies of the church were given her for expansion, for conflict, for victory. She has gone forth on the high enterprise of the world's subjugation, and she cannot stop in her onward march, or turn aside from her heaven-appointed task. Go on then, ye conquering legions of the Prince of Peace! Let no region of the habitable earth be barbarous enough or cruel enough to daunt your courageous mind! Let no opposition appal! No disappointment depress you! Know that the earth is the Lord's and the fulness thereof, and that in due time all flesh shall see his salvation.

LECTURE VIII.

CHRIST, THE BURDEN OF PROPHECY.

THERE are many distinct lines of argument, which terminate in a common conclusion, the truth of the gospel system. The exuberance and variety of these separate sources of conviction are suited to the infinite fulness of God, who hath replenished the material world with his riches, and adapted the evidences of the faith to the peculiar tastes, tempers, and intellectual habitudes of different men. Each of these sources of proof is independent of all the rest, and sufficient in itself alone.

To some, the argument which carries conviction, is the triumphant progress of the Christian faith, against early organized and incessant opposition from rival religions. Springing up among a people, naturally and universally detested by gentile nations, unsocial in their habits, of peculiar institutions, religiously segregated from the rest of mankind, in the decline of their political power and national prosperity ; in fact, a subject race, with no advantages arising from the natural abilities, the eloquence, the wealth, or the reputation of its earliest and most successful advocates, who were despised Galilean fishermen, unlearned, and laymen;* yet did this faith, mighty through God, triumph over the superstition of the people and the pride of the philosophers, the tumultuous outbreaks of the infuriated rabble, and the persecuting edicts of hostile princes—until at length, in the person of Constantine, it ascended the throne of the Cæsars.

The miracles recorded in Scripture, performed in the presence of sagacious and hostile witnesses, subjected to keen scrutiny and owned to be supernatural, occurring at intervals of four thousand years, manifest in the marvellous communications of God, with the Patriarchs, in the wonders wrought from the time of Moses to the time of Christ, and in the amazing succession of signs and mighty deeds, which continued until the close of the Apostolic age—these constitute an irrefragable argument of the divine origin of the religious system, in demonstration of which they are alleged.

Another species of proof, running back to the fall of man, and stretching onward to the second advent of Christ, when he shall come in the clouds of heaven, with the voice of the Archangel and the trump of God, to judge the quick and the dead, consists of prophecies, commensurate in duration with the history of apostate man, embracing an infinite

*Acts iv. 13. Ἀγράμματοί καὶ ἰδιῶται. See ver. 9. A. Alexander, *in loco*.

variety of minute particulars, which no human foresight could possibly anticipate or provide for, depending for their fulfilment not less on the agency of enemies than of friends, boldly committing the credit of their authors to the combinations and counsels of men widely scattered over the earth, and who were not even to be born for many generations —this species of proof which so clearly implies the determinate counsel and foreknowledge of God, is peculiarly adapted to impress another class of minds. Each of these arguments is entirely distinct from the other, and a clear addition to the other. We may consider them alone, and then each will have its separate weight, or we may consider them together, and then they will strike the mind with their collective and united force.

However we may regard the argument from prophecy, for the truth and divinity of our religion, there can be no question that the Lord Jesus himself attributed the utmost importance to it. After his glorious resurrection, we find him pointing out to his disconsolate disciples, on their way to Emmaus, the exact agreement between the prediction and the event, and showing the moral necessity for his sufferings, which existed in the purpose and prophecy of God. "And beginning at Moses and all the prophets, he expounded unto them in all the Scriptures the things concerning himself." Luke xxiv. 27–44. And he said unto them, "These are the words which I spake unto you, while I was yet with you, that all things must be fulfilled which were written, in the law of Moses, and in the prophets, and in the Psalms concerning me."

No man can read the Scriptures attentively, without remarking how solicitous the sacred writers are to show this agreement on every occasion. Hence, the expression so often used, "that the Scriptures might be fulfilled." Criminal thoughtlessness alone could induce any person to overlook the immense weight of the circumstance, on which they so strongly and so often insist. Prophecies, which but for their singular and exact fulfilment might have escaped notice altogether, are brought forward prominently to view; and so the faith of every intelligent Christian is powerfully confirmed.

Christ, considered as the burden and fulfiller of prophecy, presents the grandest subject on which the mind of man can be fixed. The wildest excursions of fancy, the most extravagant dreams of romance, are not half so amazing. It carries us back to that awful moment, when the guilty pair stood before their offended Maker, and the predestined Redeemer of a lost world was obscurely promised. It comprehends every intervening moment and each successive prophet, from that period till the day and person of Malachi. It conducts us to the magnificent courts of David and Solomon, and we see the splendours of Jerusalem, when she rejoiced in the wealth of tributary kings. Again, we wander in sadness by the waters of Babylon, and mingle our tears with those of the captive daughter of Zion. We hear Moses the man of God, whom the Jews suppose to have enjoyed more direct and intimate intercourse with Jehovah, than any other of the sons of men was ever favoured with, promising that the Lord would raise up of their brethren a prophet like unto himself. We behold men of the highest dignity, like Isaiah and Daniel, concurring in testimony with herdsmen, like Amos, and all showing what must shortly be.

Now it is the multiplicity and minuteness of these testimonies, to which I wish to direct attention; for it is in this particular point of view that the argument appears to me most complete and conclusive. It is not the meeting of a single prediction in Christ. It is not the meeting of several. It is not the meeting of many. It is the meeting of all these predictions, which assures us that Jesus is indeed the Messiah of God. In no one prophecy, in no one prophet, shall we find a full description of Christ and of Christianity. The successive revelations which were made sometimes to settle the minds of the doubtful and timid shaken by some alarming emergency in the commonwealth, the spiritual education of the chosen race, the manifold exigencies arising in the eventful history of the Jewish people, above all the clearer development of advancing time, forbade it. Before the rising of the Sun of righteousness in his unveiled glory, these prophetic teachers heralded his advent. But the general and scattered lustre which was diffused through them as a body, was collected in his divine person and shone forth with combined and concentrated beauty. Or to change the figure: no one prophet gives us a complete picture of Christianity or of Christ; no single picture could comprehend the multiplex and many-sided subject. We should rather look upon the prophets as sketchers of particular incidents and events, and upon prophecy itself as a gallery of paintings. Thus does prophecy prove itself to be from God; not because it comes as a finished picture done at one time or by one hand. It is rather a succession of pictures, executed at different times and by different hands. One presents a particular scene, incident, or object, as his birth-place. Another describes his hnmiliation. A third beholds him surrounded by the ensigns of an unenvied and universal royalty; the kings of most distant nations pressing forward to do him voluntary homage, and nations reposing in peace under his banner, and delighting to be called by his name.

These many and seemingly conflicting prophecies, uttered with the same confidence and often by the very same voice, all meet harmoniously in Jesus Christ, and assume their appropriate places in the history of the manifested Messiah. Is it wonderful, when we remember the complex and apparently discordant elements, which entered into the prophetic conception of Christ, that the prophets themselves should be represented as in amazement and searching with intense solicitude and unwearied assiduity, "what or what manner of time the Spirit of Christ which was in them did signify, when it testified beforehand the sufferings of Christ and the glory which should follow." 1 Peter i. 11. The wisdom and truth of that eternal Spirit, by whom these holy men were moved, could, and he alone could, so variously and justly describe Him, who in the fulness of time was to assume our nature and bear our sins.

Suppose a man or set of men to describe the successive periods and passages in the life of Napoleon. One might point to his birth-place on the island of Corsica. Another view him as a cadet at the military school at Brienne. A third describe his elevation to the command of the army of Italy. A fourth sketch him amid the sands of Egypt. A fifth, as emperor. A sixth, during the disastrous expedition to Russia. A seventh, amid the anxieties and overthrow at Waterloo. And the last, closing "this strange eventful history," might describe his banishment and death on the lone isle of St. Helena. No one historian could present the whole at a single view; and if he could, that view would be neither correct nor complete. Napoleon was not indeed the same man at these several periods. It is a common but egregious error, to form our conceptions of a man's character, from a survey of his finished career, and transfer this idea to any previous period of his history. But how unphilosophical, how delusive such a course! How many and often insignificant apparently, and even invisible altogether, the influences and events, which act upon character and determine our destinies!

How do our views change with circumstances and expand with success! There are those, who believe that Oliver Cromwell had the protectorate or the crown in view, when he first drew the sword against Charles the first. The same men may believe that the topmost height of his imperial elevation was clearly in the eye of Napoleon, from the beginning of his career; but such persons can know but little of human nature and of human life. In the rise of an ambitious man, as in the aspect of nature,

> "Hills peep o'er hills, and Alps on Alps arise."

This is the true history of both Cromwell and Napoleon. They could not stop midway in their career of greatness. They could not pause without receding. To ascend higher was a necessity of their position. No more could they have ventured to anticipate at first their ultimate elevation. It had been, not sagacity, but madness, in either of these extraordinary men, to have looked forward to the supreme headship of affairs, when the one was a plain country gentleman and the other a poor and obscure adventurer. The same thing is more conspicuously true of Mohammed. It is true of all men, who from obscure beginnings "achieve greatness." Their views change with their circumstances, and they rise in their aspirations and demands as they increase in power. Hence it happens that we must see them not at one time, if we would estimate them aright, but view them at each successive period, and take a comprehensive survey of their whole lives.

A similar course must be adopted by the student of prophecy. For prophecy contemplates events before they take place, as history does after. It is the part of the historian to revive the past, of the prophet to reveal the future. The man who would have an adequate idea of the wonderful variety, completeness, and minuteness of the evidence arising from the prophetic descriptions of Christ and his kingdom, must not fix his mind on any one prophecy or picture, to the exclusion of the rest; but consider each in its turn. To gaze upon this great body of prophecy is indeed like the attempt to survey the whole of a globe at a glance. While we examine one country, or even one hemisphere, we are prone to forget the corresponding portion, equally extended and equally admirable. Thus while fascinated with the minute accuracy and pathetic beauty, with which our Redeemer's sufferings are "painted out and described," we may lose sight, for the time, of the equally impressive and instructive portions, which exhibit the holy and peaceful nature of his kingdom, or those equally authentic and precious, which promise its perpetual increase and universal prevalence.

"To him give all the prophets witness." In the

promise to Abraham it is said, "In thy seed shall all the nations of the earth be blessed;" Gen. xxii. 18. And how beautifully was this fulfilled when the middle wall of partition between Jew and Gentile was broken down, and our risen Lord gave to his church her catholic commission, "Go ye into all the world and preach the gospel to every creature!" Mark xvi. 15; and what a glorious fulfilment yet awaits it, when the new song of thanksgiving and triumph shall be sung: "And every creature which is in heaven, and on the earth, and under the earth, and such as are in the sea, and all that are in them shall be heard saying, Blessing and honour and glory and power be unto him that sitteth upon the throne, and unto the Lamb for ever and ever!" Rev. v. 13. And how does history sustain the next prophecy! "The sceptre shall not depart from Judah, nor the lawgiver from between his feet, till Shiloh come; and unto him shall the gathering of the people be!" Comparing the prophecy with the fact, we find that the tribe of Judah continued as a people and possessed a government until the Messiah, and that shortly after, it lost its dominion and separate existence in the destruction of Jerusalem. In the Psalms, we have prophetic descriptions of Christ, alike in his glory and in his abasement. As early as the second psalm, the Father is represented as laughing in security and derision, at the impotent attempts of the kings of the earth, confederate against him, exalting him upon his holy hill of Zion, publicly proclaiming him the Son of God and heir of the uttermost parts of the earth, as dashing his enemies in pieces, and blessing all those who put their trust in him. In the forty-fifth, he is described as fairer than the children of men, abounding in grace, a mighty conqueror, glorious and majestic, prosperous in his enterprises, concerned for the cause of truth, meekness, and righteousness, and as its invincible champion, as having an eternal throne and a righteous sceptre, anointed above others, with the oil of gladness, rejoicing in rich and odorous garments, and attended by the Queen in gold of Ophir. His church is then described as holy and beautiful and beloved, the cherished inmate of the King's palace, adorned in fine raiment of needle-work, and as the finishing touch it is added that the King's name is everlasting. In the seventy-second, the same royal personage is described as both compassionate and just, the distinctive characteristic of his kingdom is that it is a kingdom of peace, as of his person that he is the Prince of Peace; his dominion is to be from sea to sea, the dwellers in the utmost wilderness are to bow before him, the most distant kings to bring him presents, in token of friendship and subjection. He is to be known as the friend of the poor and needy, and of him that hath no helper, and his name is to endure for ever. The hundred and tenth celebrates his deity and priesthood. All his enemies are to be subdued. His people are to be made willing in the day of his power; and his converts are to be numerous and resplendent as the drops of morning dew. In the prophecies already recited, the glory of the church is incidentally connected with that of her King. But it is more prominently set forth by Isaiah. The mountain of the Lord's house is to be established in the top of the mountains and exalted above the hills, and all nations are to flow into it. Isa. ii. 2. In the ninth chapter, we have a magnificent description of the person of Christ, in his human and divine natures.*

The passages which we have been considering present our Saviour under the character of an illustrious Prince and Ruler. There are others, however,

* The prophetic images, employed to illustrate the triumphant aspect of the Redeemer's kingdom, are well combined and exhibited in Pope's spirited verse:

Rapt into future times the bard begun,
A Virgin shall conceive, a Virgin bear a son;
From Jesse's root behold a branch arise,
Whose sacred flower with fragrance fills the skies

* * * * *

Rise crowned with light, imperial Salem rise!
Exalt thy towery head and lift thy eyes!
See barbarous nations at thy gates attend,
Walk in thy light, and in thy temple bend.

See thy bright altars thronged with prostrate kings,
And heaped with products of Sabean springs!
For thee Idumea's spicy forests blow,
And seeds of gold in Ophir's mountains glow.

equally descriptive, in which he is portrayed as poor, despised, and afflicted. One part of the prophetic portrait is not more clearly his than the other, and it is the concurrence in one person of these seemingly incompatible attributes, that establishes the truth of the Christian religion. We find these apparently conflicting statements very near to one another, and often the same writer will pass suddenly, not to say abruptly, from one to another. But that which constituted an impediment to the faith of those who studied the prophecies before their fulfilment, is a strong confirmation of the faith of those, living after the incarnation of Christ and the organization of the church. I shall of course be unable to go over the whole body of this extended testimony minutely; all that I can hope to do, and all that I shall even attempt, will be merely to indicate the argument, and refer to some of the most important passages which sustain it.

The twenty-second Psalm opens with those memorable words, which our Saviour uttered on the cross, expressive of the most mysterious and awful agonies. They can never be heard or pondered by any pious heart, without sympathy and wonder; and the record of the undeserved and unparalleled sufferings of the Lamb of God should not only make us abhor the sins which occasioned them, but should arm us to bear with unshaken constancy, our comparatively light afflictions. "My God! my God! why hast thou forsaken me?" was the prophetic and actual outcry, extorted by imputed guilt. The remainder of the Psalm is in a similar strain of sorrow, and in the minuteness of its prophecies, and in their exact fulfilment, in the recorded history of Christ, it must be regarded as one of the most important portions of the Old Testament. There are passages in the prophets, above all in Isaiah, which a tender-hearted Christian can scarcely read without weeping. The heart is softened by the consideration of what shame and grief were able to wring from the constant soul of our Saviour. In the fiftieth chapter of Isaiah, we find him using the following language: "I gave my back to the smiters, and my cheeks to them that plucked off the hair; I hid not my face from shame and spitting." The fifty-third chapter of this prophet is less like a prediction, than a historical narrative. It is, perhaps, the clearest and most complete prophecy of Christ, in all the Old Testament. The nature and object of his sufferings, as well as their fearful intensity, are there unfolded. His want of outward attractions, his lowliness and rejection, his extreme agonies, their vicarious purpose, his lamb-like meekness and resignation, the cruel injustice shown him throughout, together with the most singular circumstances attending his death, such as the guilt of those crucified with him, and the splendour of his tomb, the design of the Father in what he endured, and his glorious reward,—all these are detailed with the minute fidelity, not of a historian merely, but of an eye-witness.

We have seen what a striking contrariety there is in the prophecies relating to Christ; and yet, how exactly they are all fulfilled in his character and kingdom, his person and work. It is perfectly evident, that of the millions of men who have lived, renowned and obscure, Jew and Gentile, no other will correspond to all the parts of this prophetic picture. Of all these, there is no other, whose life history will answer to the successive pictures, presented by the ancient prophets. On the other hand, it is not less evident, that in him, the correspondence, in all points, is complete. The prophecies in the Old Testament, touching the promised Messiah, are found on comparison to tally exactly with the testimony of the New Testament, concern-the historic Jesus. The fact is undeniable, the conclusion irresistible. The Messiah of the Old Testament is the Christ of the New. Then are both Testaments given by inspiration of God. Then is the question, "What think ye of Christ?" a question of transcendent moment to every son of Adam. Then are the immortal destinies of every accountable human being absolutely dependent on the relations which he sustains, to the only Mediator between God and men—the man Christ Jesus. Then the inquiry, What must I, a condemned and helpless sinner, do to be saved? admits demonstrably of only one answer, "Believe in the Lord Jesus

Christ!" How adorable is the wisdom of God, and how clear the divine inspiration of his prophets! How do the separate rays of divine truth blend and shine in the cross of our Redeemer! How glorious are the attributes of God, providentially illustrated in the events of the life of Christ, considered in their indivisible connection with the prophecies which had gone before! How copious and clear is the proof of our holy religion, and how worthy of all acceptation the faith of the gospel!

From the ignorance, which the Jews evinced of the real meaning of their own prophecies, and their malignant rejection of their own Messiah, we may learn the disastrous effect of religious prejudice. If in the whole range of thought there be one subject, in regard to which, it becomes men to deal honestly with themselves, and obey the truth, however unexpected and unwelcome, that subject is religion. In relation to this, as to every thing else, the views which we adopt do not alter the real facts. Truth has an objective reality, an independent subsistence. It is wholly unaffected by our belief or unbelief. A man may suppose that he is taking wholesome food or healing medicine, but if through some sad mistake, he should swallow arsenic, the drug is not the less likely to be fatal. A man may go to law, under the strongest conviction that his case is perfectly just, and needs only to be fully stated to be instantly admitted, and he may find, that the very law on which he reckoned is directly against him.

A man may invest all his substance in a particular species of merchandise, anticipating brilliant and certain success, and yet want and ruin come upon him like an armed man. Truth, natural or revealed, scientific or religious, will not bend to our apprehensions; our apprehensions must bend to the truth. The great facts of astronomy, of geography, of chemistry,—we may be ignorant of them, we may deny them, but still they remain firmly fixed as the ancient heavens or the everlasting hills. The secret influences of Pleiades, the secret agencies of nature, the achievements of human art, the creations of almighty power, are not suspended on our knowledge or belief. It is not the office of faith to create, but accept revealed truth. It is like light. It bears the same relation to spiritual things that light does to natural. We might conceive the world to contain all the widely diversified objects, with which it is so richly replenished, and at the same time so shrouded in a universal pall of darkness, as to be impenetrably hidden from every eye. Now only conceive the sun to arise suddenly, in all his strength and glory; no change might pass upon a single object, and yet every thing from darkness would rise into visibility. In like manner, faith makes no change whatever in the truths of religion, or in their relation to ourselves, but in our apprehension of them. It is, indeed, "the master-light of all our seeing." It is something more than the light by which we see. It at once supplies the element and restores the organ of vision. The real difficulty, in the case of the Jews, was no obscurity in the revelation, but the veil upon their hearts in the reading of the Old Testament, 2 Cor. iii. 13–16, and when that veil shall be removed by the finger of God, they will gladly recognize the proper glory of the long-expected Messiah, the only begotten of the Father.

It is the more necessary to guard young men against the disastrous effects of religious error, because among the most prevalent and pernicious is that which supposes that God holds us responsible for the sincerity, but not for the soundness of our religious convictions. If error, on this subject of all the most important, arose simply from weakness of mind, then it is conceded that we should not be held responsible, as idiots and madmen are not accountable for involuntary ignorance or inevitable error. But it springs mainly from aversion to the truth. The corruption of the heart spreads a dark cloud over the pages of the inspired word, which otherwise would be effulgent with the light of heaven. The persistent rejection of certain truths involves a wicked and punishable blindness. The prejudice which led the unbelieving Jews to cast off and crucify the Lord of glory was unutterably wicked, because the evidence, not merely of his personal innocence, but of his divine glory, was so accessible, perspicuous, and complete. It must have been self-evident to every unbiassed hearer of his words of grace and truth, to every dispassionate witness of his works of power and love, that he was a Teacher come from God, that this was of a truth that Prophet that should come into the world, able also to save them to the uttermost that come unto God by him.

The peculiar nature of the Christian evidences affords a signal illustration of the divine perfections, especially of the wisdom and goodness of God, and a delicate test of human character. They are for the most part moral, and demand for their appreciation not so much intellectual strength and culture, as right moral dispositions. From their very nature they can be understood only by such as come to the consideration of them with candour, humility, reverence, and love of truth. To receive them in simplicity and joy of heart, there must be that inward and spiritual preparation of which the Holy Ghost is the author. The confidence of men, therefore, in their plenary and conclusive character, may vary, and in experience is found to vary, with the presence or absence, the strength or weakness, of such dispositions. The internal and experimental evidences of Christianity are those on which the soul reposes with most unshaken trust, in which the soul rejoices with most ineffable delight. No accumulation of outward evidence can be so impressive, no logical demonstration so convincing, as the direct spiritual apprehension of divine truth in its divine beauty. The truth contained in the Scriptures is intuitively recognized as the source, the standard, and the sum of spiritual excellence. We feel constrained to acknowledge the divinity of the Christian system, because it bears the image and superscription of God. There is a reigning spirit of holiness and beauty, of truth and power, in the word of God which, obviously and infinitely, transcends any thing of man's device ; and the conscience responds to the voice of its eternal and only Sovereign speaking to it from the inviolable sanctuary wherein he dwells, and with the awe-stricken disciple exclaims, "My Lord and my God !" The words of Jesus are not only superior to those of any mere human teacher, in the depth of their spiritual significance and in the strength of their spiritual sanctions; they are altogether of another kind; they belong to another sphere; they address another sense. Where the word of a king is there is power, and these are the words of the King of glory. There is no excellence which he does not inculcate, none which he does not exemplify. The noblest aspiration of the loftiest mind after glory and virtue, cannot rise above the commanded duty of every disciple of Christ. "Finally, brethren, whatsoever things are honest, whatsoever things are just, whatsoever things are pure, whatsoever things are lovely, if there be any virtue, and if there be any praise, think on these things." Phil. iv. 8.

In regard to the nature and extent of that control which we may and which we should exercise over our moral convictions, it is an unquestionable fact of consciousness, not less than of divine revelation, that we cannot indeed change our corrupt hearts, or elicit any distinctively holy affection. But we can direct our minds to some objects rather than to others, to some considerations to the exclusion of others. We can read some books rather than others. We can choose some companions in preference to others. And there are corresponding emotions awakened on the presentation of appropriate objects, and the occurrence of suitable considerations to the mind, in virtue of a law simple, universal, inevitable, the law of association. In clear addition to which, God has ordained a supernatural connection, between pious labours and spiritual blessings.

It is true, that our nature is radically corrupted, and the deadliest part of our corruption is a total inability to recover ourselves. Still we are conscious of certain moral susceptibilities, which render us the proper subjects of redemption and the meet recipients of heavenly grace. If we can do nothing directly, we can do much indirectly. If, by an immediate and sovereign act of the will, we cannot expel vicious affections, we can discard the images and ideas with which the vicious affections are naturally associated, and the Bible, which does not indeed formally propound, but silently assumes and proceeds upon the profoundest philosophy of the mind, commands us not to look upon the wine when it is red, and not to draw nigh to the door of her house whose steps take hold on death. We can direct our minds, not to the alluring aspects under which the forbidden fruit may be regarded, the sinful gratification contemplated; but dwell upon such considerations as may disarm it of its perilous power, the wrath of God revealed from heaven against all unrighteousness, the mortal misery, the incalculable mischief, which drunkenness, adultery, false-swearing, and the love of money, have produced in other cases, as revealed in inspired Scripture or recorded in profane history. We may then reflect upon the hideous evil which the particular sin to which we are tempted or inclined is, from its very nature, adapted to produce, above all the dishonour done to God; and exclaim with the purest of the ancient patriarchs, "How can I do this great wickedness and sin against God? Gen. xxxix. 9; Ps. li. 4. We may properly call to mind "in the very torrent, tempest, and whirlwind of passion," the special aggravations of the sin arising from our peculiar circumstances—age, honour, authority, family, or station.

As many of the Jews rejected the manifested Messiah from prejudice; so many stifled their convictions from fear, either for their personal safety, their property, or reputation. The evangelist John mentions some who believed on him, but would not confess him for fear of the Jews, lest they should be put out of the synagogue. Jesus himself warns his disciples against the sinful fear of men. Nothing is to be feared so much as fear, as there is no despotism so great and so harsh: none but the brave man can be free, and none but the good man can be both brave and rational. In the book of Revelation the fearful are put into the same category with the unbelievers, clearly implying the close connection between lack of faith and lack of courage, the converse of which, or the intimate connection between them, is positively affirmed by Peter, when he exhorts Christians to add to their faith, virtue, or courage—manly energy.* The relation of courage to Christianity, its proper place in a system of Christian morals, presents a subject of enquiry of vast practical moment, and one which deserves much more attention at the hands of Christian teachers, than it has received hitherto. It is, in fact, not less essential to the Christian than to the Homeric hero: and in its true nature and highest forms, it is not merely illustrated but commended and enforced in the Bible, not less than in the Iliad. In its aggressive form it is exercised principally in a positive testimony for certain truths which men are apt to despise and hate, although in themselves most sublime, and to us most needful; and a corresponding witness against certain sentiments and usages which though highly esteemed among men, are abomination in the sight of God. It commands us not to resist evil; and, therefore, many of its most despised manifestations and sublime triumphs are *passive.*

*2 Peter i. 5: ἀρετη. John xii. 42; Matt. x. 28–33.

Assuming the gentle form of charity, it *endureth* all things. In no character, is courage more useful and becoming than in a minister of the gospel: he needs it not less than a soldier. The commission under which he holds his sacred office obliges him to go to the ends of the earth, if called, in the providence of God, to visit infected districts, to minister to men dying of contagious and loathsome distempers, and confront death in all its most appalling forms. He must execute justice and maintain truth; he must exercise discipline on the rich and resentful; and thereby not unfrequently risk his reputation, ease, and what is more trying than either, the very bread of his wife and children. The highest courage is a Christian grace, and like faith and love, of which it is compounded, is to be sought from God by prayer.

LECTURE IX.

CHRIST, CONSIDERED AS OUR EXAMPLE.

We are often animated in duty simply by reflecting, how another person of eminent faithfulness would be likely to act, in our circumstances. A question which might appear perplexed, or a course which might seem doubtful, regarded alone in the light which our own reason and conscience could throw upon it, might seem comparatively clear, when considered in connection with the known principles and habits of another. There are few of us, perhaps, who have not been emboldened to enter upon a hard or hazardous career of duty, by the seasonable recollection of some one more largely endowed with faith and the Holy Ghost than ourselves. This impression will be the clearer, and the corresponding impulse the more controlling, just in proportion to the estimate which we form of the excellence and wisdom of the man, whose salutary influence we feel.

All this is not only recognized, but enjoined by the Scriptures. "Take, my brethren, the prophets, who have spoken in the name of the Lord, for an example of suffering affliction, and of patience. Behold, we count them happy, which endure. Ye have heard of the patience of Job, and seen the end of the Lord; that the Lord is very pitiful and of tender mercy." Jas. v. 10, 11. We are taught by the meek fidelity of Moses, the courageous piety of Joshua, the religious candour of Caleb, the heroic daring of Gideon, the early faith of Samuel, the elevated devotion of David, the matchless wisdom of Solomon, the steadfast resolution of Mordecai, and the wonderful patience of Job; by the affectionate reverence of John, by the impetuous zeal of Peter, by the comprehensive wisdom, the enlightened zeal, the single-eyed self-devotion, and the all-conquering vehemence of Paul. The timely recurrence of these names to memory, may well animate our souls with dauntless courage in circumstances of danger, and inspire them with heavenly wisdom when perplexed with doubt and difficulty. If we can bring ourselves to think, as they in our situation would have thought, to feel as they would have felt, and do as they would have done, we shall, in the vast majority of cases, think, and feel, and act, as we ought.

But after all, these were men of like passions with us, eminently holy, and faithful, and wise, but stained with the same original corruption, struggling with the same evil propensities, and sometimes, alas! overcome by the same temptations. We must, therefore, scrutinize their conduct with jealous vigilance, and imitate their actions with discriminating wisdom. As inspired by the Holy Ghost, their official teachings are authoritative and infallible; but as men compassed about with infirmities, their example was imperfect, as they themselves bear witness. Rom. vii., *passim;* and 1 John i. 8. With every reasonable abatement, however, on the score of their personal deficiencies when brought to the standard of a perfectly holy law, still the contemplation of their character is eminently fitted to edify and ennoble us; and it can as little be doubted that the more perfect their example, the more instructive and the more delightful to behold it. Now what was confessedly wanting in them, his personal attendants, his inspired apostles, his most saintly disciples, is found in Christ himself. He and he alone has left us an example of holiness, in feeling, in principle, in speech, and in action, which we may imitate without exception and without error. "He was holy, harmless, undefiled, and separate from sinners." When assaulted by Satan, that foul fiend was made to feel that he had no part in him, that in his nature was no corruption or weakness, on which his diabolical engines could play, on which his diabolical subtlety could fix or fasten; and the glozing tempter was forced to retire from the conflict baffled, beaten, ashamed, exposed. Our Lord's triumph over Satan in his temptation was not only in all points an example to believers, but an achievement for them. He was their federal head and representative in victory, as Adam in the fall; and as in Adam's fall they fell, so in Christ's steadfastness they stood, in his victory they conquered. Therefore, this was symbolic and prophetic of the final triumph of all believers over Satan and sin, death and hell. To others, the Holy Ghost was given by measure, to him without measure. Others were sons of God by adoption and by grace, he was the Son of God by the possession of a divine nature and from all eternity. In doing as the very best of his servants have done, we may do wrong; in following his blessed example, it is impossible to err.

Taking only a general and distant survey of the character of Christ, we behold in him the divine law fulfilled in all its demands, and obeyed in all its precepts. Matt. iii. 15. The life of the Lord Jesus Christ shows how beautiful the life of man can be on the earth. "God is light, and in him is no darkness at all." The natural sun, glorious as it is, still hath its spots, but the moral excellence of the Lord Jesus Christ is absolute, unspotted, infinite. It is the righteousness of the great God and our Saviour. But for our better instruction, certain notes of this peerless harmony are singled out—certain rays of this sunlike glory, certain features of this perfect beauty—and receive specific and significant names, that we may bestow upon them a more distinct and intelligent consideration. Thus the titles of the Lord Jesus Christ may be viewed in their intrinsic or absolute significance, in their relation to him, as marking off or shadowing forth some special aspect of his universal excellence; and in their relation to us, as indicating the attribute which we are specially to study and copy. As the Lamb of God, the sheep dumb before his shearers, we have not merely the great fact of his sacrificial oblation, but he teaches us meekness, forbearance, long-suffering, gentleness, all the passive virtues. They are designedly illustrated in these events of his recorded history. So the title of the Lion of the tribe of Judah may teach us the opposite, and not less important class of virtues, zeal, aggressive courage, strength of will and, to sum up in a word, all the active virtues. The Bright and the Morning Star indicates that as in his glorious person all divine perfections meet, so the rising of the beams of his grace upon the nations chases away the shades of night, and heralds the coming day of knowledge and holiness, of love and joy. As a painter contemplates the mien and features, the dress and gait, the fugitive aspects and expression of the person, whose portrait he desires to take; so the Christian should dwell with studious and delighted attention on the character of Christ, until the various lineaments are traced on his own soul. In proportion to the clearness, the exactness, and the beauty of the image of Christ drawn on our hearts, is the perfection of our subjective Christianity. If a man have the spirit of Christ, he will have the same spirit of prayer, of patience, of gentleness, of meekness, of active goodness, of zeal for the glory of God, indifference to unjust and unreasonable censure, invincible calmness under contumely, and provocation, and sinful persecution, which Christ himself evinced.

In his example was gathered a bright assemblage of all the graces which constitute a perfect character. In him there was no defect and no redundancy. One virtue is never exercised at the expense of another. It is this admirable harmony of excellencies, which we are especially to note and to imitate. All things great are simple—the sky—the sea. On account of this very simplicity, perhaps, we are less struck with the character than we might otherwise be. There are no salient points, the whole is a boundless and beautiful horizon. There are no peculiar virtues, there is throughout the harmony of absolute and infinite perfection. On every occasion he said exactly what was wise, he did exactly what was right. Never in the prosecution of an important object, or the rebuke of a reigning sin, or the correction of a prevalent evil, is he even for a moment betrayed into any species of extravagance, or does he for a moment overlook or forget any portion of the vast circle of human duties; but with the eye of Omniscience he scans it all at once. Surveyed in the clear light of truth, as present to his soul and shining in his life, every duty appears in its proper magnitude, and assumes its just relations. He gives to Cæsar, the things which are

Cæsar's, and to God, the things which are God's. Of him alone, of moral teachers, can it be truly affirmed, that his precepts and practice perfectly agreed. Whatever he recommended to others, he did; whatever he condemned, he forebore. And of all the abuses of his times, none pained him more, or excited in his benignant bosom deeper detestation, or called forth from his compassionate lips a more withering anathema, than did the cruel hypocrisy of the Pharisees of the day, who bound on men's shoulders heavy burdens, which they themselves would not so much as touch with the tips of their fingers. It is impossible to contemplate such a character with faith and love, and not receive the highest spiritual profit. Nothing indeed is so apt to redeem the soul from the curse of grovelling propensities, and raise it to God, as the devout and delighted contemplation of the brightness of the Father's glory, and the express image of his person in human flesh. The mind is unconsciously, but powerfully, affected by the objects on which it dwells with sympathy and delight. The forms of beauty and of grandeur which fill the chambers of the soul gradually become a part, not of its furniture, but of itself; like the burnished and brilliant cloud which we have often seen dissolving insensibly away, until entirely blended with the blue sky. So well known is this principle of our nature to poets and artists, that they love to reside amid the noblest forms of nature, or the most wonderful achievements of art. They gaze on these glories with congenial delight, until the spirit which they breathe, and the beauty which they bear, have passed into their own souls, and become a permanent portion of their spiritual being. The sacred Scriptures explicitly recognize the operation of this principle, when they urge us to behold the glory of God in the face of Jesus Christ, till we are changed into the same image from glory to glory, as by the Spirit of the Lord.

To copy the character of Christ, will require of course a very particular knowledge of the events of his life, the places which he visited, the persons with whom he was brought into contact, the occasions on which he spoke and did the things recorded of him. In order that we may have a fixed and infallible standard of duty, we must have an exact and extensive knowledge of what our Lord did, and how he thought and acted ; and with this perfect pattern compare our own thoughts and deeds in the various exigencies of daily life. Christ was the great Reformer, not in the sense of adding anything to the divine law, but of exposing and condemning the false glosses of the Jewish doctors and restoring it to its original integrity and lustre. Thus most fine gold, become dim, may be burnished and brightened. As an illustration of these spiritual reforms, we may consider our Lord's doctrine in relation to the proper treatment of enemies ; the ground and extent of forgiveness ; and the duty of suffering for righteousness, sake; all of which was exemplified in his own personal history, in infinite perfection.

The doctrine which he delivers in regard to the proper treatment of our enemies is peculiar to revealed religion. It is agreeable to reason, and it commends itself to every man's conscience in the sight of God, as truly noble. But it is not the spontaneous dictate of our corrupt affections, and it is a doctrine totally unknown to the schools of heathen moralists. With them it was a point of honour to avenge every injury, and they regarded it not as the glory of a man to pass by a transgression, but as the mark of a mean and craven spirit. But our Lord makes the cordial forgiveness of those who have injured us the indispensable condition on which we are to hope for pardon from God. He has embodied this benign principle in that beautiful prayer, which he gave as a legacy and model to his people, and we cannot say, "Forgive us our trespasses as we forgive them that trespass against us," without suspending our own pardon on the pardon which we accord. Nay more, it may be logically looked upon as a special imprecation of the awful vengeance of Almighty God, to pray for forgiveness if we fail to exercise it.

The principle on which we are required to forgive, is that God is Judge alone, and that to assume to ourselves the work of recompensing evil, is an audacious invasion of his judicial prerogative. It is in effect to displace the Deity, and act on the principle of atheistic independence. We may further reflect that it is entirely unreasonable to hope for the remission of such a debt as we all owe our Lord—ten thousand talents, while unwilling to forgive the comparative trifle due to us from a fellow-creature. The method by which we shall most successfully resist the strong impulse which hurries us on to vengeance, is calm and Christian meditation. We may regard an enemy in our thoughts, as the heartless and high-handed aggressor, who has invaded our dearest rights and offended our deepest sensibilities, or wrongfully deprived us of some coveted good; and while we give place to thoughts like these, a bitter and a burning rancour will take possession of our souls, which nothing but an ample vengeance can satiate. Or we may contemplate this very person, and all his deeds and designs of malice toward us, as an offender against that great and dreadful Being, who has made and will judge both him and us. We may think of the deep-seated and tumultuating sorrows of the heart that is capable of such perfidious and cruel wrong, and thus the correspondent feeling of pity will be awakened, and we shall be so far in spirit from the fiendish desire to torment him before the time, that we shall sincerely ask God to forgive and bless him. No disposition is more unbecoming a professed follower of Jesus Christ, than a cold and sleepless, and snake-like malice. " Put on therefore as the elect of God, holy and beloved, bowels of mercies, kindness, humbleness of mind, meekness, long-suffering, forbearing one another and forgiving one another, if any man have a quarrel against any; even as Christ forgave you so also do ye." Col. iii. 12, 13.

In the life and death of our blessed Master, we have the most sublime exhibition of the fulfilment of all these precepts. Betrayed by one friend, denied by another, deserted by all, assaulted by a furious multitude with swords and staves, confronted by false accusers, beset by a hideous combination of the chief priests and elders, condemned as a blasphemer, spit upon, buffeted, scourged, arrayed in a scarlet robe in bitter mockery, his brow encircled with a crown of thorns, reviled by the passers by, scornfully taunted when hanging on the cross, not a murmur of indignation or resentment escapes his lips. "But when he was reviled, he reviled not again, when he suffered he threatened not, but committed himself unto him that judgeth righteously," and even amid the provocations and the agonies of that hour, was heard a voice, that pierced the heavens, "Father, forgive them, they know not what they do." Luke xxiii. 34.

We have seen the generous compassion with which our Lord forgave his enemies, even at the very moment when he was enduring the utmost that their insane malice could devise or inflict. Let us consider another part of this universal goodness—I mean his tender affection to his friends, and above all to his mother. It has been objected to Christianity, that it nowhere inculcates, in express terms, the duties of friendship, with how much candour and justice we shall be able to see after passing under review a few incidents of our Saviour's earthly history. To speak of this affection, however, as the proper subject of precept or command, is to betray utter ignorance, both of its nature and office. Friendship is a sentiment which arises unbidden in the mind, on the perception of attractive qualities in another. It is the manifest token, and the natural fruit, of a certain indescribable congeniality of taste and temper. It is not an effect of volition, but an instinct of nature. It arises as surely from the common possession of certain moral affinities, as does the sense of pleasure from the sight of a lovely landscape, or from the odour of a rose. Christianity, therefore, does not institute or command, but exemplify and consecrate these beautiful regards. It is no part of our duty to feel the sentiment of friendship for any particular person, and, therefore, it is not authoritatively demanded. There are other affections, however, such as gratitude and esteem, which are often confounded with friendship in the popular apprehension, and which frequently do terminate in it, which we ought to exercise, and which therefore, are embraced in the precepts of Scripture. We are plainly required to cherish feelings of cordial good-will toward every human being, whether a foreigner or countryman, and to testify our good-will by acts of substantial kindness. We are expressly taught to be courteous, to exercise ungrudging hospitality, to show mercy to the poor, and to forgive our enemies. So far as the exercise of the emotion of friendship is a Christian virtue, it is included in the comprehensive precept of the apostle: "Finally, brethren, whatsoever things are true, whatsoever things are honest, whatsoever things are just, whatsoever things are pure, whatsoever things are of good report, if there be any virtue, and if there be any praise, think on these things." Phil. iv. 8. Friendship, as the dictate of nature and not a fruit of the Spirit, might safely be left to the simple working of nature's laws and of nature's sympathies. With the infallible insight which marks all the provisions of the gospel, our Saviour rather assumes than inculcates the exercise of this pleasing affection when he says, "If ye love them which love you, what thank have ye? for sinners also love those who love them." Luke vi. 32.

It has been very far from my intention to cast contempt upon this noble and attractive sentiment. It has always been felt with most generous ardour, with most delicate sensibility, by the purest and most exalted minds; and in its most perfect phase, it dwells only among the good. In the Lord Jesus it appeared in the highest lustre. That universal benevolence toward the sons of man, which caused him to lay aside for a season the regalia of heaven and tabernacle among us, was concentrated into a livelier glow toward certain favoured objects. It is scarcely possible to picture a more tender or a more delightful vision than that of the Son of man, retiring for a season from the crowded and splendid and wicked capital of Judea, to solace himself by a few hours' heavenly converse with the affectionate and simple-hearted family of Bethany.

The pen of the evangelist is suffused with a homefelt tenderness, while it portrays this scene of natural joy; and many a Christian household has been filled with a kindred delight, while the narrative which commemorates this scene of the moral picturesque, has been read in their hearing by some gray-headed father; and many an eye has been moistened by the tear of sympathy with Him, who, yielding to the tenderness of nature, wept with those weeping sisters. How well does this incident in the personal history of our Lord accord with the precept afterwards delivered by his apostle, enjoining it upon his disciples to weep with them that weep, and rejoice with them that rejoice!

In nothing does the divine wisdom of our Saviour appear more clearly than in his personal demeanour toward her who was so "highly favoured" as to be his mother according to the flesh. Evidently anticipating and condemning the idolatrous homage which has been bestowed upon her since his decease, he spoke of her and to her in such terms as some have deemed inconsistent with filial duty; but which subsequent events, and the present sentiment of a large portion of nominal Christendom, have vindicated as eminently wise and needful. When, upon a certain occasion, a woman broke forth into the exclamation, "Blessed is the womb that bare thee, and the paps which thou hast sucked," our Lord corrected her ignorant admiration, and said, "Yea rather blessed are they that hear the word of God and keep it." Luke xi. 27, 28. On another occasion, when told that his mother and brethren stood without, desiring to speak with him, he said, "Who is my mother, and who are my brethren?" Then turning to his disciples, he added, "Behold my mother and my brethren, for whosoever shall do the will of my Father which is in heaven, the same is my mother and sister and brother." Matt. xii. 47.

These passages plainly show that, so far from being immaculate and the proper object of religious worship to others, her own final and eternal blessedness was wholly suspended on the faith and obedience which she should render to Him who was at once her Son and her Saviour. But while our Lord did not fail to address her in such terms as should for ever rebuke idolatry, he still manifested toward her the most affecting filial tenderness. Even in that dread hour when a more than mortal darkness overspread his soul and the weight of a world's redemption bowed his head, and the propitiatory blood was flowing from his feet, his hands, his side, his brow; even then, in the last extremity of nature's anguish, the thought of her who bare him, still presses on his heart, and turning to the best beloved of all his disciples, he bequeaths the precious legacy of his mother's keeping to his fidelity and affection; saying to him, "Son, behold thy mother!" and to his mother, "Behold thy son!" What an example is here! How eloquently does such a scene enforce and enhance the sacred obligation of filial duty! How does it consecrate and endear the tender relation of parent and child! There is no spectacle dearer to the eyes of God or man, than that of an affectionate child cheering the declining years of a parent. This is evidently the order of nature and the testimony of Jesus. At such a period, life requires every sweet and soothing attention, and the emotions of complacent and gratified affection which such kindness excites, are scarcely less to be considered than the substantial services which gave them birth and being in the heart.

And if there be a human tear
From passion's dross refined and clear,
'Tis that which pious fathers shed,
Upon a duteous daughter's head.

The extreme copiousness of our Saviour's example, extending to every branch of human duty, renders it difficult to consider it at once with brevity and profit. We have already contemplated his treatment of those two great classes—his enemies and his friends. We may now glance at certain of his extraordinary works, and, in conclusion, mark his exemplary performance of the special duties which man owes to God.

It must be obvious, that in some particular aspects of his conduct, Christ could be no example to us, in consequence of the peculiarity of his person and office. We are evidently unable to follow him, when he walks upon the sea, as on dry land; when he but speaks a word, and its raging billows subside; when he converts a few loaves and fishes into an abundant supply for above five thousand men, besides women and children; when he restores the loathsome leper to perfect soundness; when he causes the sweet light of heaven to gladden eyes long sealed in darkness; or when with perhaps a more impressive majesty, he speaks and his voice pervades the silent halls of death, and recalls to the blessed consciousness of life, those who had been locked in the mysterious slumbers of the grave.

Destitute of the Divinity which dwelt in his human nature, as in a temple, we cannot, of course, imitate these miraculous manifestations of love. But we can exercise the principle from which they all sprang, and which they were all designed to express. It is true, we cannot raise the dead, but we can serve the living. We cannot cleanse the leper, but we can visit the fatherless and the widow in their affliction. We cannot by miracle supply the needy, but we can take of our abundance and minister to their wants. We cannot restore sight to the blind, but we can ourselves "be eyes to the blind." We can sit by the bedside of the blind and sick, and read the words of grace and life. Thus, though we cannot exercise His almighty power, we may practise his fervent charity; and if there be in us the same mind which was also in Christ Jesus, we shall, like him, go about doing good.

The narrow-minded and unbelieving consider that lost which they dispense in charity. They look upon it as water spilt upon the ground which cannot be gathered up again, as just so much taken from the sum of their possessions; whereas nothing is so truly and permanently ours as that which we bestow in Christ-like charity. "He that giveth to the poor lendeth to the Lord; and that which he hath given will he repay him again." "Blessed is he that considereth the poor; the Lord will deliver him in time of trouble." "It is more blessed to give than to receive."

Surely it was not without design to affect our hearts with a kindred charity, that the record of our Saviour's personal beneficence was made. Surely, it was not without design to awaken in us a kindred compassion, that we are informed of the bag set apart for pious alms, even among the indigent attendants of our Lord; and if on a bed of death —a scene that most of all needs the balm of pleasant memories—and a scene too, from which the most beneficent life will look sufficiently barren of good; if on a bed of death any recollection would be sweet, it must be the thought that others, who have gone before us to God, have borne witness to our bounty, and that there are those left behind us on earth to attest it when their praise can no more delight "the dull, cold ear of death."

In Christ, we perceive the harmonious union of the active and contemplative life. His beneficence toward men was not more remarkable than his piety toward God. If he went about doing good to the bodies and souls of men, he walked with God in the secret path of spiritual service. In religious observance, his example was as instructive as in useful labours. He often retired from the companionship of his friends to commune with his heavenly Father. Not one of his disciples spends the time in prayer which he was wont thus to employ. He spent whole nights in prayer. Alone with his God, by the cold mountain's side, with no couch but earth, and no canopy but heaven, he poured out his heart in prolonged supplications and pious praises. In the garden of Gethsemane, on the Mount of Olives, on the bloody cross, he prayed in agony and tears. And in these hours of sacred and dread striving with his God, against principalities and powers, he did not confine his prayers to his own personal deliverance, but bore, on his burdened heart, the sins and the sorrows of all his people. As by virtue of his intercession it was, that Peter's faith failed not, and he was graciously recovered from his grievous fall; so the steadfast faith, and patient piety, and triumphant struggles of his people since, are due to the prevalence of the same intercessions. In the seventeenth chapter of John, we have a recorded specimen of our Saviour's intercessory prayers. We there behold his reverence, his trust, his thankfulness, his goodness, his faithful love to his own people, his wise concern for their welfare, his comprehensive and enduring care for all the generations of the just.

This is a part of his perfect example, which especially commends itself to our imitation. Without the spirit of prayer, there can be no Christian piety. It is a blessed privilege of the believer in Jesus to resort to him for light in darkness, consolation in trouble, courage in danger, deliverance in temptation, and triumph in death. All his people have experienced the efficacy of prayer. They have gone forth from their dwellings in the anticipation of trial, with a mind sobered and strengthened by the grace of Christ. And when the archives of eternity shall be explored, and the events of this life known in their hidden springs and most remote issues, it will doubtless appear that many a noble deed and many a wise forbearance has been effected in direct answer to prayer, prompted by the Spirit and presented in the name of the Lord Jesus.

LECTURE X.

THE CHRISTIAN GRACES, THE HIGHEST HUMAN VIRTUES.

In the Christian system, the connection between religion and morality is vital. In the ancient pagan religions, and in many, perhaps in most if not in all, of the systems of modern paganism, they were entirely divorced. They were not only divorced but antagonistic. Instead of enforcing the obligations of morality, and establishing the authority of conscience, the pagan religions relaxed the one and abolished the other. They not only permitted but prescribed the grossest immoralities, in many instances making gluttony, drunkenness, and lust, a component part of their abominable idolatries. Their religious services were the deification of sin, and their sacred temples, the schools of pollution. The moral among the pagans were such not in virtue but in spite of their religion, and the mild and modest among them habitually adored cruel and licentious deities. The gods they worshipped were not gods but devils, the magnified image of their own vile affections. Such were the gods of Egypt and Syria, of Canaan and of Greece.

It is highly worthy of remark that all corruptions of the true religion and all departures from it, may be traced and measured by their immoralities of theory and practice; teaching that we may do evil that good may come, cheat and lie and murder for the credit of the church and the glory of God, and indulge the lusts of the flesh and of the mind, provided we attend rigorously to all purely religious duties.

This misdirection of the religious sentiment, this divorce between the religious instinct and practical virtue, which is the common characteristic of all false religions and of all perversions of the true, is perhaps the greatest enemy of true piety and of pure morality. The exclamation of Madame Roland, when she was carried to execution: "O Liberty! how many crimes have been committed in thy name!" may be applied to religion. Looking back upon the records of history, beholding the shameless impurities, the horrible profaneness, the senseless mummeries, and the hideous cruelties, which have been employed in the worship of God, the bloody wars which have been waged for the suppression of his truth and for the extermination of his servants, we may well exclaim, "O Religion! what crimes have been committed in thy name!"

Such is the connection between religion and

morality in the pagan and in the corrupter forms of the Christian religion. But in the pure and Apostolic draught of Christianity, religion and morality are not indeed identified but inseparable. Religion is the animating soul, morality the outward and visible body. The Christian religion, having its seat in the soul, works from within outwardly, and the daily beauty of a good man's life is only the outward shining of a beautiful soul. It is the unveiling of the hidden and holy light within, the ebullition and overflow of the inner fountain of life, the efflorescence and bloom, the aroma and sweetness, of the incorruptible seed sown in the heart and growing up silently and secretly there. It is the ointment of the right hand that bewrayeth itself, the articulate and audible voice going forth from the recesses of the invisible oracle. In the wise and beautiful words of Coleridge, in whom the wisest philosophic subtlety and the richest poetic fancy were so signally combined: "It is indeed faith alone that saves us, but it is such a faith as cannot be alone. Purity and beneficence are the *epidermis*, faith and love the *cutis vera* of Christianity. Morality is the outward cloth; faith the lining. The images of the sun in the earthly dew-drops are unsubstantial phantoms; but God's thoughts are things; the images of God, of the Sun of righteousness, in the spiritual dew-drops, are substances, imperishable substances.*

* Literary Remains, &c., Vol. v. p. 463: Prof. Shedd's Edition.

A man who is truly religious will be righteous just in proportion as he is religious. Practical excellence is not only the fruit and the token, but the test and the measure of Christian piety. It is its felt accordance with what conscience, the voice and vicegerent of God in the soul, declares, demands, and recognizes, as true, as fitting, as august and holy and divine, which constitutes the plainest and strongest of all the manifold proofs of the divinity of the Christian religion, as revealed in the Scripture and represented in the Saviour. We cannot but feel, and from the depths of our spiritual nature own, that a system which appeals so clearly and so powerfully to that spiritual nature, in its wants and wishes, in its hopes and fears, in its highest aspirations after truth and beauty and goodness, is a true revelation from the true God. The voice which comes forth from these holy oracles, is echoed back from the profoundest depths of conscience. That religion, which is felt to affirm, to exalt, and to enforce all the sanctions and all the obligations of the purest moral virtue, is felt to be true and divine. It is self-evidencing, shining in its own light, and commending itself to every man's conscience in the sight of God.

No other than the true religion ever could accord with an enlightened conscience. In every other there is a perpetual conflict between the convictions of the moral sense and the supposed will of God. The only strife which can arise in the mind of a

Christian is that which arises out of a want of complete correspondence between his religious creed and his moral conduct. He feels that he fails in the attainment of perfect excellence, only because he fails in perfect obedience to what his religion requires him to be and to do. The peculiar power of the doctrine of Christ over the hearts of men lies in the profound consciousness, that when most under the dominion of the Christian faith, they are most under the dominion of moral virtue. The purifying efficacy of the Christian faith on himself is a consideration which addresses itself with most intense force to the consciousness of every believer; and it is, of all the arguments for the divinity of the Christian system, the most simple and conclusive. When most religious we are most virtuous. When our souls are glowing with most grateful and adoring love to Him, who though he was rich yet for our sakes became poor, that we through his poverty might become rich, we feel the most patient and zealous love for all men, especially for the household of faith; and thus there is consciously established the most complete correspondence between Christian doctrine and moral excellence.

It is a sad and notorious truth, however, that many nominal Christians, losing sight of the distinctive glory of their heaven-descended faith, really sever their religion from their morality, almost as widely as the pagans ever did. They go to church and pass through all the forms of worship punctually

—it may be punctiliously. "And they come unto thee as the people cometh, and they sit before thee as my people, and they hear thy words, but they will not do them: for with their mouth they shew much love, but their heart goeth after their covetousness." Ezek. xxxiii. 31. "To what purpose is the multitude of your sacrifices unto me? saith the Lord: I am full of the burnt offerings of rams, and the fat of fed beasts; and I delight not in the blood of bullocks, or of lambs, or of he-goats. When ye come to appear before me, who hath required this at your hand to tread my courts? Bring no more vain oblations: incense is an abomination unto me; the new moons and sabbaths, the calling of assemblies, I cannot away with, it is iniquity, even the solemn meeting. And when ye spread forth your hands, I will hide mine eyes from you; yea, when ye make many prayers I will not hear: your hands are full of blood. Wash ye, make you clean." Isa. i. 11–16.

It may be that these deluded men have, while in the house of prayer, what they account comfortable frames and feelings, and yet when they go back to their homes and their business, are just as proud and selfish, and passionate and niggardly, as they ever were. Thus they do practically "fix a great gulf" between religion and morality, an ordinary day and the Sabbath—the counting-house or the workshop, and the sanctuary. Their religion and their every day morality, like knowledge and wisdom, "far from being one, have ofttimes no connection,"—like oil and water they refuse to coalesce; the one floats on the top, the other sinks to the bottom.

The heartfelt reception of the Christian religion carries with it not only the cardinal virtues—such as truth, justice, chastity; and the utter abhorrence of the opposite sins—such as murder, lying, theft, and all manner of uncleanness, but the finer, loftier, and more ethereal graces, are studied and striven after, not only the sterling virtues that go to make up the web and the woof of the Christian character, but the beautiful graces which set it off and commend it; sincere goodness showing itself in its own native and proper lustre. According to one divine delineation of the Christian virtues; Phil. iv. 8; we have first the broad foundation of truth, underneath the whole structure as a solid rock, on which the whole building with its appropriate ornaments and pendants may firmly and fitly rest; then what is honest, or, perhaps more strictly according to the present sense of the terms, what is venerable or holy, and likely to fill the beholder with involuntary awe, but with an awe so tempered by the presence of what is graceful and lovely, as to be altogether pleasing—next justice or equity in the dealings of men one with another, seeking not to overreach or injure—manifestly formed on the golden rule of doing to others, as we would have them do to us, and illustrating what this same apostle enjoins elsewhere: "Look not every man on his own things, but every man also on the things of others,"—then purity, not only unfeigned purity of heart, but showing forth in speech and action,—"the sun-clad power of chastity," in Milton's majestic phrase. These are the foundations and main supports of the building, the solid rock, and the strong pillars, and the great pilasters; to these we are to add every embellishment, and every attraction proper to the finished beauty of the finest Christian character. Whatever will naturally conciliate favour and win esteem, whatever men justly approve as amiable and praise-worthy, must lend its fascination and its charm to the Christian character, must confer a glory and beauty on this architecture of heaven.

This is an inspired sketch of what every Christian is sacredly bound to aim at for himself, and as far as may be, to embody and illustrate. He is not only to abstain from the grossness of positive pollution, but to avoid what is unseemly or doubtful. He is not only to attain the solid and staple principles of the Christian character, but the cheerful and shining courtesy which will put a lustre on his substantial worth and give it currency. How many are there who are good at heart, men whom the better you know them, the more you respect and like them; but men who are rough and regardless of appearances, whose very piety has something dogmatic and repulsive in its manifestations, whose good is evil spoken of, not in consequence of any essential defect, but from the neglect or disdain of the amenities of life! There are truly good men whose dialect and demeanour do not recommend their religion, especially to the young and unthinking men, who are seemingly so sour and cheerless and churlish, so obviously lacking in that courtesy which the most energetic and uncompromising of the apostles explicitly commends, in that winning sweetness of manner which is the true index and fitting interpreter of a loving heart, which propitiates a brother offended, and so disarms opposition, often before it be itself aware, that they fail to recommend their religion, where they might and when they ought.

So far is this gentle consideration for the rights and feelings, and even the innocent prejudices of others, from involving a sacrifice of principle, or implying a lack of honesty, that it is impossible, utterly impossible, for any who have not beforehand secured the substantial framework, the strong and solid foundation of love and truth and goodness, to feel or to evince it. These external indications then appear as their fitting garments, their goodly and graceful ornaments, apples of gold in pictures of silver, the spacious and solid temple but stately and magnificent, " Doric pillars overlaid with golden architrave."

Thus we find that throughout the realms of nature and the works of Providence, the useful is accompanied by the beautiful; the beautiful is based and built upon the useful; from the sublime mechanism and movements of the heavenly bodies, so glorious to behold, the moon walking in brightness, accompanied by troops of stars, her shining retinue, to the modest flower which performs her part in the chemistry of nature, and in the very act unconsciously unfolds her beauty to the eye, and the rich ripe fruit, or the clusters of the vine, bending beneath their precious burden, while glowing with beauty and fragrant with sweetness.

A character, which should exhibit the graces portrayed by the pencil of the Holy Ghost, would shine in the native beauties of holiness, in the genuine colours of heaven. What is holiness, but the incarnation of the gospel in man, the possession of the Spirit, and the practice of the precepts of Christ? What is holiness in the creature, but likeness to the all-glorious Creator? And what is the beauty of God, but the general sum of his ineffable and adorable perfections in their harmonious manifestation? The beauty in which man shone at first, consisted in the image of God, in knowledge, righteousness, and true holiness, with dominion over the creatures. That image lost by the apostasy, is restored in redemption; forfeited in fallen Adam, is replaced in the Redeemer Christ.

To effect this renewal, the everlasting Jehovah laid his glory by, became man, and suffered the death of the cross. He thereby purchased for his own people the precious gift of the Holy Ghost, whereby they are supernaturally renewed in the image of God, and have a title to the inheritance of heaven. The crown of knowledge, holiness, and dominion which had erewhile fallen from their heads, is restored again by the gracious hand of a sovereign Redeemer. They have now pardon of sin, peace of conscience, hope of a blessed immortality, and the promise of a glorious resurrection. It is enough to say in the words of an apostle, "Even now are we the sons of God, and it doth not yet appear what we shall be, but we know that when he shall appear we shall be like him, for we shall see him as he is: and he that hath this hope purifieth himself, even as he is pure. If ye love me, keep my commandments." This is the all-comprehensive test of love to the Saviour and of fitness for the kingdom of heaven.

The improvement of a truly regenerate person in all the beautiful graces, which adorn the Christian character, is a gradual thing. There is first the grain, then the ear, after that the full corn in the ear. The path of the just is as the shining light, that shineth more and more unto the perfect day. The building rises gradually and gracefully toward heaven. There is first the foundation, then the main body of the building, then the capital and crowning ornaments, the roof overarching all, and the spire pointing to the skies. At first, the image is drawn, it may be only in obscure outline; but afterwards the lines are deepened, the features become more distinct and definite, and the resemblance to the divine original clear and strong.

The pulsations of spiritual life in the hearts of those who are nevertheless "born again, not of blood, nor of the will of the flesh, nor of the will of man, but of God"—may be so faint and feeble that they themselves may be scarcely conscious of it; but the proper law of the kingdom of God, in grace as well as in nature, is growth. We are commanded to "grow in grace, and in the knowledge of our Lord and Saviour Jesus Christ." We are exhorted to add to our "faith virtue, [or courage,] and to virtue knowledge, and to knowledge temperance, and to temperance patience, and to patience brotherly-kindness, and to brotherly-kindness charity;" and we are divinely assured, that "if these things be in us and abound, they make us that we shall be neither barren nor unfruitful in the knowledge of our Lord Jesus Christ." Faith is the root-grace, the mother-grace, because it apprehends Christ, from whose indwelling Spirit all other graces flow. Love is the flower of all the other graces, outlasting faith and hope, flourishing in immortal fragrance and beauty, when transferred to the atmosphere and transplanted in the soil of Paradise. These graces are essential to the Christian character in its lowest stage of development, so essential that a man cannot be a Christian and have them not, yet they are capable of glorious increase. And as such, they are matter of precept and promise. "Add to your faith," says

Peter, in a passage already quoted. "Lord, increase our faith," is the prayer of the apostles. Paul prays for the Colossian Christians, "That they might walk worthy of the Lord unto all pleasing, being fruitful in every good work, and increasing in the knowledge of God;" Col. i. 10; and for them of Thessalonica, "The Lord make you to increase and abound in love one to another, and toward all men." 1 Thes. iii. 12.

We may now very briefly indicate some of the most important instruments which Providence employs in this beauteous building, to bring it to the fullest symmetry, and adorn it with the fairest lustre.

It is an assured and delightful truth, "that all things work together for good to them that love God; to them that are the called according to his purpose." The way of the Christian is divinely ordered in all things. The gracious providence of his God hedges him about at all times. Every event in the earthly history of God's elect, is preordained and rendered conducive to their abundant entrance into the everlasting kingdom of his dear Son. In reference to their present afflictions, it is particularly promised that they shall work out for them a far more exceeding and eternal weight of glory. Temptations, which are so dreadful in the view of our personal weakness, and are so fatal to great multitudes of the rash and self-confident—are to them not merely harmless, but just occasions of thanksgiving and joy. "My brethren, count it all joy when ye fall into divers temptations; knowing this, that the trial of your faith worketh patience." James i. 2, 3. Thus the secret *nexus* between the adverse dispensations of God, and the spiritual prosperity of his people, is disclosed; and so the sharpest sting of sorrow is extracted.

All the spiritual mercies of God are directly designed, as they are visibly adapted, to form and fix his holy image in their hearts. The ordinances of his house, the prayers, the praises, the instructions, and the sacraments of the sanctuary, are formed in infinite wisdom, to the end that they may build us up in faith and hope of the gospel. Every exercise of these graces tends to increase and confirm their dominion. The presentation of the gracious and majestic objects of our faith to the mind, the distinct and delighted contemplation of them, has, naturally, a powerful tendency to awaken, to extend, and to purify the Christian graces, to which they severally and unitedly appeal. Superadded to all this is the supernatural supply of the Spirit of grace: "He giveth power to the faint; and to them that have no might he increaseth strength. Even the youths shall faint and be weary, and the young men shall utterly fall: But they that wait upon the Lord shall renew their strength; they shall mount up with wings as eagles; they shall run and not be weary, and they shall walk and not faint." Isa. xl. 29–31.

Every thing spiritually good in fallen man is, in Scripture, ascribed to the supernatural working of the Holy Ghost; and the experience of all Christians tallies with this account. Pure religion and undefiled is implanted, nurtured, and brought to fruitfulness, by constant supplies of the Spirit of grace. For in us, that is in our flesh, dwelleth no good thing; "and without *me*," says our blessed Saviour, "ye can do nothing."

There are times when the ploughman is called to plough and sow, for then the earth is soft with showers and ready for the seed; so there are times when the soul should be cultivated with special diligence, for it is softened by affliction, and humbled by sorrow, and made susceptible by grace. There are times when men should make great progress in the understanding and fear of the Lord, in the abundance and fervour of their supplications in the Spirit; in their contempt of the pleasures, and dreams, and passions of the world, and in the warmth and purity of their love to the Lord Jesus.

The necessary conclusion from all that has been alleged, touching the design of God's providential dispensations, and his spiritual mercies, is, that the continual growth of all true believers in the knowledge, the favour, and the likeness of God their Saviour, is both a privilege and a duty. But here we are met with a practical difficulty. We often hear good men bemoaning themselves, and saying, "Oh that it were with me as in months past, when the candle of the Lord shone upon me! My leanness! my leanness!" When these sad complaints proceed from the sincere servants of the Most High, they are generally the outcry of a conscience wounded and writhing under a sense of sin. They have forsaken God and fallen from their first love, and as a punishment, he sends a horror of great darkness. If a Christian is not growing in all the parts and perfections of the Christian life, he ought to be sad, he ought to be in trouble, and it is a dark sign of hypocrisy if he is not in trouble, while living far below his recognized duty and revealed privilege.

But some may complain that they are making little, if any conscious progress, while yet they are following on to know the Lord—faint, yet pursuing. To such, I would suggest, in the first place, that they may be really making progress, and yet not be able themselves to discern it. This view, of course, is not to be applied by any who are living in known sin, or who are at ease in Zion, but by the humble, the self-distrustful, the conscientious. Let such reflect that the operation of grace in the heart is mysterious, and it may be imperceptible, yet we know that, though unseen, the progress is not the less real and rapid. "Though," says the apostle, "our outward man perish, yet our inward man is renewed day by day." 2 Cor. iv. 16.

We may not be able at the close of any one particular day to perceive that we have made any appreciable advance, but take a longer period and the progress may be more apparent. Thus, when we look at a young tree, or a flower, or a stalk of corn, or a growing child, at the close of a single day, we are able to detect no difference in height. But let weeks or months intervene, and then the growth will be obvious enough.

In the second place, we should reflect that we may be growing in humility and godly sorrow; in circumspection and in conscientiousness, in spiritual discernment and in Christian charity; when we are not growing in conscious joy, and in a comforting sense of the divine favour. We may, notwithstanding, be better in the sight of God, when we are worse in our own; and we may be better in the sight of God, because we are worse in our own.

We should have ever present to our minds a high ideal of Christian excellence, not to discourage, but to stimulate us. This ideal we shall never approach unless we use, with all diligence, the means graciously afforded. They who neglect the means need not expect to attain the object. Is it surprising, then, that so many among us languish, when they do so little for their spiritual health and happiness? Do we expect a man to enjoy bodily health who neglects all rational precautions, and plunges into every species of excess? You may reply, If we are absolutely dependent upon divine grace, for every good gift, where is the use of giving ourselves any trouble about the result? Why be so concerned about diligence on our part? It might be enough to reply, God wills our diligence and commands it. We are exhorted to "give all diligence, to make our calling and election sure." 2 Peter i. 10. That should be enough for us. But the method by which God works in us, is by inciting us to work. He works in us both to will and to do of his good pleasure; and every deep conviction of the necessity of using to the utmost all the appointed means of grace, is the fruit of his Spirit and the pledge of his favour.

The religion of Jesus, in its power and purity, is the perfection of human nature—its glory and crown. The grace of the Lord Jesus Christ is the universal cure for the manifold maladies, the only corrective of the deepseated evils, of human nature. It does not, indeed, alter or abolish the individual differences among men, so as to reduce them all to one level, to raise them all to one rank, to cast them all in one type. But it makes the most of any one individual, on whom its power is legitimately exerted, that can be made of him. It educates, while it exalts all his powers, enlarges and fills all his capacities for truth, and goodness, and happiness. All men have not the original grant of power, which was lodged by nature in the Apostle Paul. But take a common man and let him be possessed of as large a measure of grace as was bestowed on this gifted disciple of Gamaliel. He might not then be as ardent, as wise, as industrious, as eloquent, as useful as he; but still he would be an eminent saint, a hero, a light, and if need be, a martyr. He would be altogether a different man from what he was before, he would seem to have new faculties. Nothing so elevates the moral feelings and invigorates the natural powers as true piety. It strengthens, feeds, developes, disciplines, and purifies all the powers of thought and action. A thorough Christian is of necessity a thorough man. Let any ordinary man be transformed by divine grace into a thorough Christian, be filled with the Spirit, and he will at once undergo a wonderful metamorphosis; he will become at once a marked man and a mighty man; retaining all that properly pertains to his own individuality, he will yet be obviously a different man, and a man in every point and particular, in mind, and heart, and life, incomparably elevated, thus showing that the Christian graces are the highest human virtues.

LECTURE XI.

THE GLORY OF GOD, THE END OF OUR EXISTENCE.

THE glory of God, or the manifestation of his supreme excellence, may without irreverence be declared to be the ruling thought of the divine mind, the principle and end of his government, to which every thing is subordinated, to which every thing is referred, the original spring and ultimate object of all his counsels and dispensations, word and works. We therefore as his creatures should set it before us, designedly, consciously, habitually, as the motive and end of all we do. "To the glory of God," should be written on ourselves, on all our possessions and on all our actions. If we ever forget that this is the ultimate end of all that he does or permits to be done, we lose sight of the central and controlling principle of the divine government. It is to the moral what the attraction of gravitation is to the material world. To it every thing is subordinated and on it everything is dependent. For it we should be resolved to live, and prepared and content to die. Our minds, our lives, will never be rightly adjusted, until they are brought into conscious and complete harmony with the mind and counsel of God.

Obedience is the end of all scientific theology; we know truly only so far as we love and serve. There is a theology of the intellect, cold, barren, dead, that may be united with a proud, imperious and selfish temper, and there is a theology of the heart, warm, fruitful, living, full of mercy and good fruits, gentle, loving, faithful, self-sacrificing, promoting universal goodness, the fruit of God's truth, applied by his Spirit, and the sure token of his everlasting favour. 1 Cor. viii. 1. That knowledge which has its residence only in the head and on the tongue, is of all ignorance the most incurable and pernicious. Obedience to God is first active, doing whatever he commands; secondly, passive, forbearing to do what he forbids, and patiently enduring what he imposes. Our constant prayer should be, Lord, make me fully obedient to thee in all things through the life-giving power of thy grace! We misplace and misspend our anxieties, on earthly treasure and pleasure, instead of our souls and heaven and God. He who does nothing without reference to the glory of God can never willingly commit sin. How would the thorough ascendency of this principle simplify our course and sanctify our lives! How would it project our thoughts and aims out of ourselves! How would it raise them in sacred strivings above the stars of heaven! We should put no limit to our obedience and consecration, not seek to come up to some commandments or to the faithfulness of some Christians, but seek to do all the holy will of God, spiritually and perfectly. We should set no period to our labours, but be most diligent and devoted, for the time to come, in those very things in which we are conscious of failure in the past, multiply defences and forces at the weakest points, be strong in the Lord, and in the power of his might.

There is great danger, as we advance in life, of confounding the maturity of natural powers and the soberness incident to a more enlarged experience, with growth in grace. As there is a weariness of life altogether different from deadness to the world, so there is a perception of many of its vanities, and a conviction of many salutary truths, painfully inwrought, which is consistent with a state of mind, subject to all worldly delusions and practical ungodliness.

Duty and devotion rest on the same foundation. Both are meant to render honour to God. To abstain from pettishness, violence, and all unseemly actions and emotions; and to practise all righteousness, therefore, is as needful as to pray. The consideration of the future, as an incentive to prayer, is wise and Christ-like. The habit of taking trouble on trust is most unmerciful to ourselves and the source of unprofitable despondency, wholly foolish so far as we are concerned, and at once betrays and begets lack of confidence in the providence and perfections of God. But there are certain inevitable and awful events before us all, doubtless some peculiar trials in reserve for some, that should be so considered as to cause us to prepare for them by prayer. The Bible tells us even in prosperity, to remember the days of darkness, for they shall be many.

In a time of adversity, Moses thus prays, "So teach us to number our days that we may apply our hearts unto wisdom." Our Saviour generally, specially in the immediate foresight of what was coming upon him, persecution, betrayal, denial, death, and such a death! fortified himself by prayer, and so should we. Prayer is our strength. Who has not felt it a secure retreat when every other refuge failed; a fortress of God safe and impregnable, because it engages omnipotence to aid us? It lays hold of every ground of hope, every perfection of God, every promise of Scripture, every motive of action. The real source of independence of men is dependence on God. Faith is the antithesis and antidote to fear. When we can confide the whole care of our souls, the whole conduct of our affairs, to God's keeping, they will be safe and we shall be happy. But they who renounce the service of God in prosperity, when they think themselves secure, will forfeit and must forego his help in trouble, when they feel themselves needy. We should not transfer to any creature or created cause, the love and confidence due to God. If in danger or trouble, we trust in strength of body, or wealth or health or intellect, and they fail us, we have nothing left us and therefore fall into despair. When we lose them we lose every thing; but when we put our trust in the living God, we confide in One who will never leave or forsake us; and if we lose every thing else, we have all things in him. Ps. lxxiii. 25. Faith in God implies and embraces all things, confidence in the efficacy of prayer, sense of protection in peril, comfort in distress, hope in extremity, perpetual watchfulness against temptation and sin, together with unslumbering diligence in all Christian duties. No man ever yet attained great moral elevation, without faith in God and the spiritual strength which is derived from communing with him in prayer. It is the highest triumph of faith, to believe that God will overrule all the evil in the universe to the best and noblest end—his own glory. And of this we may be absolutely certain, from the knowledge not only of his purposes, but of his perfections, his wisdom, holiness, power, mercy, goodness, and truth. To love God and to trust in him when he deals kindly with us is natural, and may be seen even in the heathen; but to love him when he deals with us in fatherly severity, argues a truly Christian and heavenly temper.

No creature is mean, since every creature can minister, and was made to minister, to the honour and glory of God. Man is especially noble as capable of rational, spiritual, and voluntary service, and of conscious delight therein. The differences between all human souls are small, compared with the things which they have in common. Varieties of endowment, of vigour, versatility and brilliancy of mind—of education and accomplishment, vast as they may be—are yet inconsiderable, compared with their common curse in the apostasy, their common redemption in Christ, and their common immortality in a future state of being. This constitutes the real basis of the dignity of man, as man, of the immeasurable importance of every human being, savage and civilized, bond and free. The importance which attaches to mankind is quite peculiar. The interests of the universe centre around man. Our planet is small in comparison with others, but it is the battle-field of the Deity and the devil, the scene of the apostasy, and the theatre of redemption. No man can be considered altogether wretched, so long as he retains his interest in his fellow-man. Hamlet was on the verge of distraction, or over it, when he said, "Man delights me not." Brotherly love is the medicine of individual griefs, as well as the cement of human society. To cultivate a generous interest in our kind, to cherish a tender spirit of humanity, is not only to perform the most comprehensive of our social duties, but to do most for the development and purification of our own happiness. The devil can do us no greater mischief, than to make us first hate God, and then hate man.

From the hour a man first believes, every thing

should be given to God, and every thing should be done to God, and for him. So comprehensive is the apostolic precept, "Whether therefore ye eat or drink, or whatsoever ye do, do all to the glory of God." 1 Cor. x. 31. Whatever we undertake, and whatever we do, we are to do all so that God shall be praised and his glory promoted. This principle, as it is of the utmost importance, so is of the widest compass. It extends to every person and to every thing, to every action and to all places. Nothing can be so important, and nothing so trivial, as to be exempted from its operation or beyond its range. In every prayer we offer, in every letter we write, in every book we read, in every journey we take, and in every conversation in which we engage, there should be ever present and ever active the desire to glorify God. We ought ever to contemplate and contrive every thing, with an eye to its effect on our own, and the spiritual interests of others. In thinking, in speaking, in feeling, and acting, our sole and simple purpose should be to glorify God. If every Christian were fully possessed with this habit of mind and life, how speedily would the world be converted to God!

There are two ways of doing all to the glory of God; one is explicitly, consciously, designedly. This we do in the important actions, and on the great occasions of life, when we first solemnly dedicate our souls to God, and sanctify our lives to his holy service. We do this designedly and of set purpose to his honour and glory. So when we unite in any act of formal divine service, as in the solemn celebration of the sacraments, and in the stated service of the sanctuary, or in the regularly returning seasons of private devotion.

But, as Christians, we may, we should, we must set the Lord always before us, and feel that because he is at our right hand, we shall not be moved. We may not only pray formally and statedly, but always, without ceasing, never fainting. Thus, we may prosecute the glory of God, habitually, unconsciously, and generally, in the spirit and habit of the soul, in every action of the life, and during every hour of the day. It is possible to pursue our common occupations in a sacred spirit, to intersperse secular labours with fragrant and holy prayers, to send up silent ejaculations to God, like swift-winged messengers of grace, thus keeping up an instantaneous and uninterrupted commerce with the glorious world of invisible spirits. So to live, is to have every day sanctified, a perpetual Sabbath of the soul!—"the bridal of the earth and sky!"

Thus, a real Christian will see God at all times, and serve him in all things, in his recreations, and in his engagements. To him, a common meal, sanctified by faith and thanksgiving, will yield more spiritual nourishment than a sacrament, to many others. This, to use the beautiful thought of the excellent Leighton, is the *elixir* that turns lower metals into gold, the meaner actions of this life into obedience and holy offerings unto God. To maintain such a holy correspondence with heaven, amid our earthly labours and distractions, would lighten them amazingly, and make them sweet. This, again, to adopt Leighton's thought, would refresh us in the hardest labour; as they that carry the spices from Arabia are refreshed with the smell of them in their journey. 1 Peter iv. 2, 3. Religion is not intended for high days and holidays only, but for all days. It is not intended to afford us holy cheer and comfort in death only, but to be our law, and guide, and rule in life as well. It doth not carry with it a recompense only, but a duty and a service also. It is perfectly possible to pursue a sacred calling, and be engaged in sacred duties in a secular spirit; as on the other hand, it is possible to pursue a secular business in a sacred spirit, with faith and prayer, referring every thing to the will, the providence, and the glory of God.

After these more general views let me now suggest some specific reasons why we should make the glory of God our ruling principle and final aim in life. To have some great and worthy object in life is infinitely needful to every rational creature. And what should this object be but to glorify our Creator, from whom we have received, and from whom we hope all things? What nobler object can any one propose to himself than to live for the glory of God? How mean and little that man's spirit, whose supreme concern on earth is to advance his own selfish interests, to heap up money, to build up a family, to make a name! Compare an evangelical missionary of education, ability, piety, and zeal, who spends his life in leading the heathen to heaven; instructing them kindly by the wayside and from house to house; sanctifying their heathen tongue by the translation of the Christian Scriptures, with the same man spending his life in his native land for merely personal purposes, or going to the ends of the earth for the sake of gain. How exalted the one! How common-place the other! The one, how like a white-robed visitant from heaven, passing through this world of ours to beautify and bless it! The other, a son of our common clay, born to consume the fruits of the earth, and die and be buried and forgotten! What a noble answer is given to the first question in our shorter Catechism! "What is the chief end of man? Man's chief end is to glorify God and enjoy him for ever." What end can the soul propose to herself more lofty and seemly, more religious and holy, more attractive and wise, than the beholding and manifesting the supreme glory of the ever blessed God, the infinite Creator of heaven and earth, to all eternity? What can impart such dignity, interest, elevation, sobriety, steadfastness, and usefulness to our daily life, as the faithful pursuit of this sublime end? What else can save us from a life of insipidity, insignificance, failure, wretchedness, and vice, but such a ruling principle, such an ultimate and exalted aim? What is the reason that so many men are perfect blanks, utterly and inexpressibly useless in the world, vegetating rather than living, therefore not cared for, not respected while they live, not missed nor mourned when they die, unless it be by some fond mother or sister, whom the

"Strong bond of blood or nature draws,"

to weep over the grave where the useless lie buried? Why is it that so many are positively pernicious, their presence a pollution, their example a pest, their memory a shame, and their influence a curse? Why is it but because they have not lived to the glory of God, they have never once raised their eyes above "this dim spot which men call earth," to the bright and imperishable heavens, because they have never sought seriously, diligently, patiently, prayerfully to serve the great Creator and our Saviour Jesus Christ? These men have lived for meaner, lower, sinful, selfish objects. They have been of the earth, earthy. They have loved and served the creature rather than the Creator, who is God over all blessed for ever more. They have lived and longed and laboured for the things of time and sense, not for the sublime realities of faith and eternity, for the glory of God, the favour of Christ, the fellowship of the Spirit, and the happiness of heaven. Therefore their whole career has been one grand mistake, one general failure, one deadly sin. They have been their own beginning and end, centre and circumference. Their thoughts have begun, continued, and ended in self. Themselves have been their God. They have been atheists because they have been egotists. Their idolatry has been the basest and the vilest, the idolatry of self. They have denied the Supreme God because they have been devoted to their own glory, or to their own ease, or selfish enjoyment. The busy aspect and pompous preparations of such men, men who live for temporal and selfish objects merely, men who in heart and in fact are worshippers of self, may be fitly likened to an Egyptian temple of enormous size, of immense cost, but enshrining an ape or a toad.

All men, who are not living to the glory of God, are living for self. All who are not faithful, self-denying, earnest-minded, single-eyed Christians, are living for self. Their real object may be artfully concealed or disguised, and from no human eye more effectually than from their own; but if they are not living for this great end, if they are not guided by this great principle, if they are not animated by this high purpose—regard in all they do to the glory of God, nothing, alas! can be plainer than that they are living for themselves. The first reason then why every man ought to live to the glory of God, is that every man ought to have a great and governing purpose; to give unity, consistency, elevation, and interest to his life; to prevent aimless and useless endeavours, ill-directed, unfixed, wandering desires; to evade the restlessness, the perplexity, the anxiety consequent on an ungoverned mind; and as every man should have a governing object in life, that object should be the worthiest and highest. And the worthiest and highest can be nothing less, can be none other than the glory of God. A second reason for making the glory of God the principle of action and the end of existence is, that thus and thus only shall we attain the proper perfection of our nature. The mind is a proper end unto itself. Knowledge is so noble and so precious, because it builds up the soul in strength and freedom and dignity, not mainly for any inferior and outward advantages connected with it. "But the greatest error of all the rest (says Lord Bacon) is the mistaking or misplacing of the last or furthest end of knowledge; for men have entered into a desire of learning and knowledge, sometimes upon a natural curiosity, and inquisitive appetite; sometimes to entertain their minds with variety and delight; sometimes for ornament and reputation; and sometimes to enable them to victory of wit and contradiction, and most times for lucre and profession, and seldom sincerely to give a true account of their gift of reason, to the benefit and use of men; as if there were sought in knowledge a couch whereupon to rest a searching and restless spirit, or a terrace for a wandering and variable mind to walk up and down with a fair prospect, or a tower of state for a proud mind to raise itself upon, or a fort or commanding ground for strife and contention, or a shop for profit or sale, and not a rich storehouse for the glory of the Creator, and the relief of man's estate."*

Sir William Hamilton, in his Lectures on Metaphysics, just issued from the press, a book that opens a new world of thought to the intelligent student, remarks more directly and explicitly on this point: "It is manifest, indeed, that man in so far as he is a mean for the glory of God, must be an end unto himself, for it is only in the accomplishment of his own perfection, that as a creature he can manifest the glory of his Creator. Though, therefore, man, by relation to God, be but a mean, for that very reason, in relation to all else, is he an end."†

God has so constituted man and the universe which he inhabits, that he can find his true dignity and blessedness, only when supremely devoted to his service. It is the crowning glory and felicity of man's nature, that he has been made capable of knowing, and loving, and serving the true God and Jesus Christ whom he hath sent. He was never designed to find his happiness in the creature, but in the ever blessed God; in a life of selfish ambition, of vain power, of successful striving after worldly riches, or glory, or good, but in seeking

* Advancement of learning, Bk. 1st. p. 174. Montague's Edition.

† Metaphysics, p. 4.

after God, in the adoration of his glorious perfections, in profound subjection to his sovereign will, in a sweet sense of his gracious nearness to us, and fatherly compassion toward us.

If romance be an extravagant and erroneous estimate of things, if it be a departure from the truth of nature into the wild realms of fancy and fiction, then is the cold, hard, scheming man of the world—intent on multiplying possessions which he does not need and cannot use—as unwise as a romantic boy. For consider, how little it takes to satisfy the natural needs of men, how insatiable are artificial and imaginary wants, how this man is degrading his nature, hardening his heart, burdening his conscience, and blotting his memory, merely that he may indulge his imagination by dwelling on that wealth, which he never means to use. The romantic boy and the scheming man are equally busied with day-dreams and air-castles; who shall say, whose are the more rational, or rather the more ridiculous? It would not be hard to say, whose are probably the more exalted and generous; since a tincture of noble sentiment is apt to mingle with the extravagant dreams of youth, and impart to them a beautiful colouring.

The true riches are not material, but spiritual; they do not consist in fertile fields, and stately dwellings, and fine pictures; in delicious viands, and costly wines, and a long train of obsequious attendants; but in a well-ordered mind and a pure heart; in composed affections; in a clear judgment; in a candid soul; in a will resigned to the dispensations of heaven, and resolute in the choice of right; in the absence of envy, suspicion, and hate; in the presence of humility, charity, and goodness; in the favour of God, which is life; and in his loving-kindness, which is better than life.

A transforming change, in the inner character of the soul, would alter even the outward aspect of the world. Then smitten with the sacred love of truth and goodness, spiritual beauty and heavenly wisdom, how empty and insipid would seem the ordinary objects of ambition and desire! how like painted vanities and gaudy toys! The object of the Christian religion, subjectively considered, is the purification and development of man's inner and spiritual being in the glorious service of God. The essence of this consists in the assimilation of the soul of man to the image of God, in knowledge, righteousness, and true holiness. In these spiritual treasures the proper wealth of the soul consists; and thus we find that the perfection of our nature is inseparably blended with the service and glory of God.

A third consideration, directly leading to the same conclusion, has been incidentally alluded to already; but, for its importance, deserves to be more formally propounded. It is, that his own glory is the ultimate end of all that God does. If his own glory be the highest object that he can set before himself, if it be the end of all his dispensations, it is clearly the highest object which we can propose to ourselves. And need I argue, to prove to any man who has access to the Bible, that this is, of a truth, the ultimate end of all the dispensations of God? Is not the whole Scripture from beginning to end, one long, repeated, and diversified testimony to this effect? "The Lord hath made all things for himself." "For of him, and through him and to him, are all things." "For it became him, for whom are all things, and by whom are all things." "I am Alpha and Omega, the first and the last." Prov. xvi. 4; Rom. xi. 36; Heb. ii. 10; Rev. i. 8.

The ultimate end of the creation, then, is to show forth the glory of the Creator. In every star his glory shines, in every stream, in every flower and gem, in every insect, in every angel, in cherubim and seraphim, in heaven and on earth.

We cannot honour God by giving to him any thing that he has not already in possession, but we may honour him by acknowledging what he is, reposing confidence in his promises, regarding his threatenings with awe, and giving to him the glory due unto his name.

The glory of God is the end contemplated in the whole course of his providence, and pre-eminently, in the work of redemption by our Lord Jesus Christ. At the birth of our Saviour the angels sang, "Glory to God in the highest, and on earth peace, good will toward men." "That at the name of Jesus every knee should bow, and every tongue confess, that Jesus Christ is Lord to the glory of God the Father." "Having predestinated us to the adoption of children, to the praise of the glory of his grace." Luke ii. 14; Phil. ii. 6–11; Eph. i. 3, &c.

The glory of God is the end of the creation, the end of providence, the end of redemption, of his judgments on the wicked, of his sanctification of the righteous. It is the great end of the miracles which he has wrought, and of the ordinances which he has bestowed upon his church.

In strict correspondence with this declared design, is the structure of our Lord's prayer; the first petition of which is that his name be hallowed, and the conclusion of which is an ascription of glory to God, "for thine is the kingdom, and power, and glory, for ever, Amen." That which God aims at we should aim at, that which the God and Father of all proposes to himself as the best and highest end of all that he does in nature and providence, in time and eternity, on earth and in heaven, by angels and men, should be our chosen aim and end.

This doctrine lies at the foundation of all correct theology, of all just views in speculative morality, of all sound principles of practical morality, of all philosophic truth, and of all wise legislation. Regarding his own glory as the final aim of all his dispensations and decrees, many difficulties in the course of divine providence, otherwise insuparable, disappear at once; and many vaunted improvements in systems of philosophy, morality, and law, are perceived to be false and hollow. Much of the philanthropy which is supposed to be Christian, is, in fact, antichristian, opposed alike to the law and the gospel, equally irreconcilable with the spirit of the Mosaic and Christian dispensations. Thus, those views of morality and law which resolve all punishment into benevolent chastisement for the good of the offender, and represent the sole purpose of suffering judicially inflicted to be for the prevention, and not the punishment of crime—are opposed alike to the instincts of conscience, to the dispensations of God himself, and to the welfare of human society. Much of the humanitarianism of this age and country rests upon a total misapprehension of the true character of the divine administration, and is wholly inconsistent with any high view of human obligation, and of human destiny.

LECTURE XII.

THE PROVIDENCE OF GOD IN THE COMMON AFFAIRS OF LIFE.

THE Bible is an inspired commentary on the dispensations of God. It lifts the veil from divine providence and shows his agency where, otherwise, it might not be seen or suspected. There is an incident in the history of Israel, which is in this point of view peculiarly instructive. Joshua x. 11. The Hebrew leader had been engaged in a perilous conflict in defence of the Gibeonites, his allies and dependents. The enemy far outnumbered any forces that he could bring into the field. But, animated by the justice of his cause and putting his trust in Israel's God, he advanced suddenly upon the enemy and gained a decisive victory. Now, in the inspired account of this engagement, the agency of God is recognized throughout. It is the Lord that discomfited the foe before Israel; the Lord that slew them; the Lord that chased them; finally it is the Lord that cast down great stones from heaven upon them, causing their dispersion and death.

If an uninspired historian had been giving a narrative of this battle, he would probably have done it in this wise: "The courage and conduct of this skilful and intrepid leader were crowned with deserved success. His enemies, confident in their superior numbers and anticipating an easy victory, were surprised, subdued, and scattered. What contributed not a little to the success of the forces of Israel, was a fortunate fall of hail, which blinded and terrified their adversaries." If the writer were a philosophical historian, like Hume or Gibbon, he would probably add, with a sneer, that "the discomfiture of the allied forces was the more disastrous and complete, by reason of a natural phenomenon which their ignorant and superstitious fancies interpreted as a token of the displeasure of the gods."

What a difference would it make in history, if it were written and read and acted under a perpetual sense of the divine presence! Practically, the majority of men are atheists in their way of thinking, or they conceive every thing to be subject to an iron necessity; the universe to be governed by blind mechanical forces, alike uncontrollable and irresistible, which they are content to recognize under the dignified designation of "the laws of nature." They thus contrive to banish God from his own universe as effectually as from their hearts, to depose him from his kingly throne, or reduce him to a pitiable impotence and inaction.

If this be philosophy, we would none of it! We prefer to believe with the simple-hearted Christian, who, taking the Scripture for his guide, can sing with cheerful faith that beautiful hymn,

> In each event of life, how clear,
> Thy ruling hand I see:
> Each blessing to my soul, most dear,
> Because conferred by thee.

God speaks of this world as his world. He claims it as his own. He declares his presence in every place, his agency in every event, his power over every person, his sovereign sway over every department and every manifestation of nature.

God speaks his will in his providence, he does not write a man's sin over his name, but he so sends his punishment as to mark the man and to mark the sin. How often is all this perfectly plain, especially when the outward deed is shone upon by the faithful light of conscience, and most of all, when conscience has been itself first shone upon by the pure light of God's truth and Spirit! It is each man's business to find out his sin for himself, and so to read God's providence as to rise from the lesson a wiser and a better man. If *we* do not see the hand of God in the events of daily life, it is our own blindness and folly. His awful voice is heard not less distinctly, not less impressively in providence than in nature; in the calamitous events of life, not less than in the strife of the material elements; in the shocks and troubles of the heart, not less than in the angry tones of the thunder; while his gentle power is felt in the sweet peace of the soul, not less than in the beautiful sunshine and the soft evening breeze.

It is thus that God rules in nature, in history and in the ongoings of the world. He does really rule as much in profane as in sacred history, but not so manifestly. The veil is removed in the one case, it remains in the other, to conceal "his hand and his counsel," however, only from the unbelieving and the undiscerning. How gloriously did Jehovah of hosts, the King of Heaven, go forth of old at the head of his armies! How often, how solemnly, with what authority does he declare that they got not the land in possession by their own sword; neither did their own arm save them; Ps. xliv. 3; but his right hand and his arm and the light of his countenance, because he had a favour unto them; that the horse and his rider were thrown into the sea, by the Lord Almighty, when Pharaoh and his "Memphian chivalry," sank like lead in the mighty waters! The pillar of cloud and of flame was the token of the God that led them. The stars in their courses fought against Sisera. The proud hosts of Sennacherib, King of Assyria, were gathered together against the beloved of the Lord, and he sent forth an angel and slew in one night a hundred and eighty and five thousand.

Like the leaves of the forest, when summer is green,
That host with their banners at sunset were seen;
Like the leaves of the forest, when autumn hath blown,
That host on the morrow lay withered and strown.

In the times of the Judges, it was the Lord God of Israel, that triumphed by Gideon, by Jepthah, and by Sampson.

In the life of David we have repeated illustrations of the same fact. It is written, "Saul sought him every day, but God delivered him not into his hand." 1 Sam. xxiii. 14. Without admitting that the evil actions of men proceed permissively from God, and are comprehended in his plan of moral government for this world, and are overruled so as to advance his ultimate and gracious designs, we can not interpret Scripture or deal with the facts of human history. Not to insist at present on the most important and illustrious instance, the condemnation and crucifixion of the Lord of glory, we can not but be struck with the testimony of David, when urged by Abishai to suffer him to slay the injurious and blaspheming Shimei. It is abundantly manifest that Shimei's cursing was the "foaming out" of diabolical wickedness, in itself altogether unprovoked and inexcusable, and of course an affront to the holiness of God; and yet David, in the exercise of meekness, humility, faith, and wisdom testifies, "Let him alone and let him curse, for the Lord hath bidden him." 2 Sam. xvi. 11. The following chapter clearly shows that the impressions made on our minds in the exercise of reason, by advice offered, are equally under the dominion of providence. The counsel of Ahithophel would have been fatal to David. It would have secured the throne to Absalom; and he and his counsellors were at first unanimous in the opinion that it should be adopted. But the Lord had determined otherwise, and accordingly he is moved to call in Hushai. And even to us the counsel of the latter seems quite as probable and far more safe. At all events it was followed, and the purpose of God accomplished in the swift destruction of the unnatural and rebellious son. 2 Sam. xvii. 14. "The king's heart is in the hand of the Lord; as the rivers of water, he turneth it whithersoever he will." Prov. xxi. 1.

Now, in the ordinary course of God's dealings with nations and with individual men, his providence is not less wonderfully at work than of old. But we have not the hand of the divine Revealer to lift the veil. God works most when he is least thought of. All the elements are under his control; he sends the winds out of his treasury; he calls to the lightnings and they say, "Here are we!" "He giveth snow like wool; he scattereth the hoar-frost like ashes;" Ps. cxlvii. 16; he rules over the apparently lawless waves of the sea; he tells them when to rage, and when to be calm as a sleeping infant. There are times when a great moral purpose is visibly accomplished by a seasonable and striking movement of the elements, in which the agency of God is as undeniable, as immediate as it was in the annals of ancient Israel. In the dispersion of the fleets of the Spanish Armada, proudly called the Invincible, who can deny that the hand of God was as plainly revealed for the preservation of the true gospel in England, as it ever had been for the confusion of the idolatry of Baal or of Ashtaroth? Who but the Lord of all the earth raised that tempest, which scattered the ships of Spain, confounded the counsels of the Pope, and dashed the hopes of Philip? Who but God alone? And let us, American freemen, never forget that more than once, in the darkest hours of our Revolutionary struggle, God appeared as our helper and guardian. Just when the bravest began to fear, and the most sanguine to despond, some seasonable and surprising turn would take place in our affairs, plainly marked with the finger of God. And he who observes that most remarkable movement in its causes, course, and consequences, in the passions and errors, which precipitated it, in the marvellous meeting of happy contingencies in its progress, and its unforeseen and even now incalculable results, cannot but adore the wonder-working providence of God.

The ancient Greeks greatly erred in multiplying divinities, assigning its peculiar deity to fountain and shade, to land and sea, to earth and air, to the household and hearthstone; and yet there was a great truth underlying this superstition. The truth was the all-pervading, ever-active, every where present providence of the one living and true God. We should learn to recognize God's providence in the familiar history of families and individuals. But how stupidly blind are we for the most part! God sends sickness, but he is little thought of. We can explain the operation of second causes. We can show the connection between our exposure to the sun, our imprudence in diet, our over exertion of mind or body, our excessive and wasting anxieties, and the visitations which followed. But we cannot see the hand and counsel of God in the matter. Now, if the Bible were to write the history of the case, how different would it seem, how differently would it sound! It would then be God that sent that sickness, God that saw fit to try you with those inward, disquieting fears, God that caused you to undergo those violent fatigues; for the Bible makes him the Lord of sickness and health, of life and death. Not to own the hand of God in these daily events, is not philosophy but unbelief. It is rank impiety. It is absolute atheism. Who denies the operation of second causes? Not the Scriptures most assuredly. But they affirm the sovereign rule of providence over them, his infinite wisdom in ordering and bounding them, in the accomplishment of his gracious purpose in them and by them. God takes away a son or a father, but the veil is not lifted. You can see to a certain distance. You can understand the operation of certain visible causes, certain material agencies. But every man's life has two histories, a secret and an open. Every event has two interpretations, a material and a spiritual. It may be all true, that your son or your father died, in consequence of certain remedial agents being neglected, or postponed, or inaccessible, in consequence of a certain state of the atmosphere concurring with a certain state of the system, which developed or induced disease. But why stop there? All this an atheist might own. A Christian believes much more; he rejoices to think that *beneath* and *behind* this veil of second causes, of visible and material agencies, there was an invisible and intelligent agent at work, and that agent, his almighty Friend, his heavenly Father. Is there anything unreasonable in such a creed? anything delusive or unworthy in such comfort?

It is to those of us who hope and trust in God, a truly delightful thought, that he can make not only the marked and memorable events of life conduce to our salvation and redound to his glory; but the small trials, the petty vexations, the insignificant provocations and perplexities. Filial confidence in the providence of God is essential to happiness in a world like ours, full of mystery and change. And a Christian's cheerfulness depends very much on the objects of his habitual contemplation. If a man look, first and most, at the number, force, malice, and subtlety of his enemies, the various difficulties in the way of his ultimate salvation, he may well be despondent. But let him look at the perfections, promises, and providence of God, at the person and work and grace of the Redeemer, at the steadfastness of the covenant and the fulness of the Spirit, and he may well hope and rejoice. The strength of the everlasting Jehovah is mine, because I can lay hold of it by faith and prayer. We are especially to admire the wisdom of God in his methods of providence and in answering prayer. He is revealed in Scripture and known in experience to answer "the effectual fervent prayers" of his pleading people, even while they are ascending to heaven, as in the case of Daniel, Danl. ix. 20–27; on the day of Pentecost, Acts ii; when the church prayed without ceasing unto God for Peter, Acts xii. 3–9; when Paul and Silas prayed and sang praises unto God, Acts xvi. 25–40. But if this were invariably the case, it would doubtless come to be looked upon, as in some way necessary and mechanical, like the ordinary operations of nature and providence. Thus the supernatural character of God's answers to prayer is kept up; and the faith of his elect vindicated and fostered.

The history of the church is the record of successive wonders, when we regard the signal and seasonable deliverances which she has experienced, as the interpositions of God. In ancient days, her apostles were supernaturally inspired with the knowledge of the truth, for her instruction and comfort. They were warned by significant dreams and visions of impending dangers, and of the best methods of escape. They were admonished by revelation, when to make a journey, whither to go, and what should be the issue of a hazardous or dubious enterprise. Acts xvi. 9, xxvii. 23; Gal. ii. 2; Acts x. xi. xv. 2. It is a very signal illustration of the providence of God toward his church, that the occasions, the scope, and the structure of the apostolic Epistles, should have been such as to afford permanent instruction, touching the most important doctrines, the most dangerous heresies, the most mischievous disorders, the most excellent graces, the administration of discipline, the duty of ministers, the obligations of men to the civil authorities, and all the relative duties, springing from the constitution of human society, and the various offices of father, husband, master, embracing and prescribing the correlative duties of children, wives, and servants.

At different periods in later ages, the divine deposit of the true doctrine has been threatened and imperilled; but God has raised up able and faithful men to define and defend it—men who could bring the pearls profoundly hidden in the depths of Scripture into open day, and clearly interpret for her own recognition and rejoicing, the common consciousness of the Christian church. Who can read the history of the apostolic conferences, and not see that they were presided over by the infallible Spirit of the living God? Who can consider the course of later and uninspired Christian councils—note the disturbing agencies at work among them, the natural darkness of the human mind, and its strange proclivity to error, and then see the clearness, the accuracy, the subtlety, with which exceedingly difficult and delicate, but withal, most precious and vital doctrines were affirmed and illustrated, were stated and established, so that all succeeding Christians have found those early symbols and confessions the best expositions of the common faith, and have been utterly unable to improve upon them, or to go beyond them; who, I say, can consider these things, and deny the supreme and gracious providence of God? The same all-wise and beneficent Being, who has furnished antidotes where poisons grow, has sent forth champions of truth to meet the teachers of error, has summoned an Athanasius to bear witness to the Divinity of our blessed Lord against the god-denying heresy of Arius, and an Augustine to vindicate the doctrines of grace against the proud and pestilent teachings of Pelagius. The same gracious providence that raised up the Apostle Paul like a pyramid of fire from the ashes of his martyr Stephen—sent forth in successive ages, fathers, confessors, reformers, and martyrs to bear witness to the truth, in a day of trouble, and rebuke, and blasphemy!

God's providence appears, in so ordering all things—the most trivial and minute, the most unwelcome and painful, things seemingly most adverse and injurious—as to secure the salvation of his chosen. His natural and gracious sovereignty over all elements, agents, events, causes, and effects, is gloriously exercised in doing just what is needful, what is wisest and best to accomplish the end in view—sending trouble when and where and in the form, in which it will be most efficacious, causing his Holy Spirit to co-operate with his providence, working within by his grace on the thoughts, the feelings, the convictions of the soul, so as most effectually to draw it to himself and bind it fast in chains of heavenly love. These chains, woven by the hand of God, are willingly worn; instead of being detested as the badges of servitude, the soul rejoices in them as her ornament and strength. "Thy people shall be willing in the day of thy power." "All things work together for good to them that love God, to them that are the called according to his purpose."

We know of no employment, more appropriate and delightful, than thus to contemplate God, executing in the whole course of his visible providence the secret purposes of his grace. And if we had an inspired interpreter of the mysteries which we meet with here, we should doubtless often discover a benevolent purpose where now all seems dark, and discern an intelligent Agent presiding over the apparently casual and capricious agencies of nature.

Even now, obscure as the dispensations of God confessedly are, in regard to particular events, yet reason and faith, enlightened by the divine word and Spirit, can suggest general considerations to console the pious under the heaviest afflictions. It is enough for us to know that God has command of all, and that he loves his people with an infinite love; therefore, we may conclude assuredly, that he bestows on them as much of all kinds of temporal good as they can bear. At the period of life which infallible wisdom judges best for them, they gain or lose, they grow rich or become poor, they are ruddy with health or are wan with pining sickness; their children and brethren are about them, or they are put away in silence and darkness. Yet whatever happens they know is for the best, so far as they are concerned. Some, it cannot be doubted, get to heaven with poverty and trial, who never would get there with prosperity and plenty. Therefore, the apostle includes death as well as life in his schedule of the saint's treasures. If we could see the marvellous means which God employs to bring men to repentance, we should be amazed. Some, as Henry Martyn's friend, by a casual reproof, the effect of which, we might have imagined, would have been quite different. The government of all men and all events is going on to gather in the elect of God.

The ultimate end of God's dealings with his own children, is to empty them of self that they may be filled with his fulness. This every believer is made at last to feel, and does in his heart acknowledge. At death and in the near prospect of eternity, he is truly thankful for bodily pains, for bodily sickness, for trouble in his family, for pecuniary loss, for disappointed hopes, if such has been their fruit, if this has been their glad and golden issue. His disciplined heart, his purified spirit says, Be thou exalted, O Lord, by me, though I suffer and die for it!

So strong is our corruption, so entrenched is selfishness within us, that this sad discipline is often sorely needed, nay, is often indispensable. Even zeal to be actively employed in God's service may degenerate into sinful impatience. We may glorify God by waiting the time his providence shall appoint. "He that believeth shall not make haste." When the cloud abode upon the Tabernacle, the children of Israel rested in their tents; Num. ix. 18; and it would have been rebellion in them to have hasted on, even to the promised land. This may comfort those who are cut off from active usefulness, and temper the rash zeal of the inexperienced.

The discipline of sorrow is to many the gateway to heaven. As a physician is obliged to keep a patient on low diet, who is consumed with a raging fever, and is often forced to reduce his system by blood-letting, so our Divine Physician of the soul is many times compelled to keep his people low by poverty, sickness, reproach, bereavement, and even the absence of a confident sense of his favour, lest they be consumed by the fire of pride, vain glory, lust, or anger. Therefore, "whom he loveth he chasteneth, and scourgeth every son whom he receiveth." The more a man is fortified by wealth, and health, and earthly good, the less direct apparently is his dependence on God, and the less sensible of it is he. These gifts interpose between the heavenly Giver and the soul so liberally supplied; and instead of leading him to worship God with discerning eye and grateful heart, they too often cause him, like the foolish king of Babylon, to glory as if they were the work of his own hands, as if he were himself God: "Is not this great Babylon that I have built for the house of the kingdom, by the might of my power, and for the honour of my majesty?" Danl. iv. 30.

Modesty in our judgments, concerning the providence of God, is intimately connected with the exercise of charity toward others, and the enjoyment of peace in our own minds. It is confessedly mysterious now. It is only partially unveiled here. But it is, therefore, the best discipline of the most excellent virtues, faith, patience, humility, forbearance, and brotherly love. As he is justly reckoned a faithful friend, who maintains the honour of his friend, not only when it is aspersed by the ignorant, the envious, and the malicious, but when it is really obscured by unaccountable conduct; so he is the most faithful friend of God, who believes and teaches that his way is perfect, even when his path is in the deep, and his footsteps are not known; and who, amid the clouds and darkness that now invest his providence to mortal ken, is still assured and still proclaims that righteousness and judgment are the habitation of his throne.

The doctrine of Providence may justly be regarded as a sort of test doctrine, the reception or rejection of which determines a man's religious character; for no doctrine is more explicitly affirmed by Christ, and none is more truly grateful to one who has imbibed the spirit of Christ. Our Saviour makes the providence of his heavenly Father to be in the moral world, what the law of gravitation is in the natural—all-comprehensive, and everywhere operating; extending to the majestic march of the heavenly hosts, and to the flower which to-day is, and to-morrow is cast into the oven; to the flight of a sparrow and the falling of a hair; and to all the interests, temporal and spiritual, personal and relative, for time and eternity, of all his people! And what more natural to a child of God, than to receive that doctrine, so full of solemn cheer, that tells him he is ever walking under his heavenly Father's eye; that wheresoever he may wander beneath the cope of heaven, he is still within a charmed circle, which that Father's gracious presence ever fills; and that, although to the uninstructed heart and to the unanointed eye, all may seem cheerless and casual, disordered and dark, it is his sacred privilege to discern the form of one like unto the Son of God, even in the furnace of affliction; and when he is made to triumph over his enemies by any visible and intermediate agency, it is his and his alone to discern the helping hand of his gracious Father! *

* It is gratifying to observe how uniformly Washington recognized the overruling providence of God, and in the most explicit terms, as at the discovery of Arnold's treason: Irving's Life of Washington, vol. iv. pp. 162, 436, 508, &c. "When I contemplate the interposition of Providence, as it was visibly manifested, in guiding us through the Revolution, in preparing us for the reception of the general government, and in conciliating the good will of the people of America toward one another after its adoption, I feel myself oppressed and almost overwhelmed with a sense of divine munificence."

LECTURE XIII.

SOVEREIGN GRACE, THE SINNER'S HOPE.

If we had a wise spirit, we should be filled with love and wonder and worship, with thanksgiving and deep gladness, in a world of beauty like this, when we look at the bright birds and hear their sweet song, and see them gracefully hopping from bough to bough, and gaily disporting themselves in the pleasant sunshine; when we see the many-coloured beauties of the skies, and the soft green of the grassy landscape, and the deep shade of the full-leaved trees. Oh! how good and loving must our heavenly Father be! Then to think, that all these are in a world of sin and woe, and that he has sent his Son to save, and to save by dying! "For when we were yet without strength, in due time Christ died for the ungodly." "This is a faithful saying and worthy of all acceptation, that Christ Jesus came into the world to save sinners." "For God so loved the world, that he gave his only-begotten Son, that whosoever believeth on him might not perish but have everlasting life." "For thy name's sake, O Lord, pardon mine iniquity for it is great." "Come now and let us reason together, saith the Lord; though your sins be as scarlet, they shall be as white as snow; though they be red like crimson, they shall be as wool." Rom. v. 6; 1 Tim. i. 15; John iii. 16; Ps. xxv. 11; Isa. i. 18.

These several passages, taken from the Old Testament, as well as the New, set forth: first, the *ground;* secondly, the *extent* of forgiveness. Salvation for sinners is in all its parts and provisions undeserved and extraordinary. From the beginning to the end, from Alpha to Omega, from Genesis to Revelation, from its first and eternal inception in the divine mind, through every period and by every process of development, it is the motion and offspring of sovereign grace. The moving cause of our salvation is in God and not in man. It is in the inaccessible and adorable depths of the divine nature, that we are to search for the *reason* and *ground* of the plan, which restores weak, corrupt, and apostate man to the image and enjoyment of God. If we wish to know *how* it is and *why* it is, that we are to be saved, by what instrument and for what cause, we must look away from ourselves and glance our eyes upwards to God. "Even so, Father, for so it seemed good in thy sight."

The petitioner for pardon is to base his plea, not on anything in himself, but only on what is in God, on God's revelation of what he is in himself, and what he has done for the sinner. On the name of

God and on that alone, the sinner is to base his hope and urge his plea. This he is to put in the forefront of all, as an ample shield, an invincible argument, an adequate answer to all objections, a final solution of all difficulties. This he is to take as a broad and strong foundation to build upon. "For his name's sake." If allowed to plant himself on this ground, the Devil himself might pray. No sinner, how great soever his sin, need fear, need despair of finding mercy, if only he have a warrant from God to use this argument, "for thy name's sake." And the only reason, why the prince of the power of the air, by whatever name known, Beelzebub, Apollyon, Satan, or Belial, cannot be pardoned and reinstated in his forfeited throne, in his lost dominion, is that he cannot pray this prayer. He cannot urge this plea. He is not permitted to build upon this foundation.

Let us proceed to survey this ground, to consider this foundation more closely. What is meant and what is said in that form of speech, "for thy name's sake?" What are we to understand by the name of God? It is a comprehensive phrase, expressing the general sum of the divine perfections. Now it is not for the glory of the divine perfections, that Satan should be pardoned. It is for the glory of the divine perfections, that he should be punished; and accordingly there has been a special, an ample, an awful provision made for his punishment, none for his pardon. For him and his rebellious crew have the deep foundations of hell been digged, fire and brimstone, which the breath of the Lord doth kindle, have been abundantly prepared. "There is weeping and wailing and gnashing of teeth," "where their worm dieth not, and their fire is not quenched." Mark ix. 46. There no love, no light, no mercy, no mitigation, not a moment's ease, not a moment's respite is ever known; but only terror, and darkness, and remorse, and wretchedness, and ruin, and despair, whatever is known or dreamed of or possible, whatever men imagine of wild, and horrible, and loathsome, and hideous, and hateful, is there. And it is there expressly for him and for such as are like him.

"Then shall he say also unto them on the left hand, Depart from me, ye cursed, into everlasting fire, prepared for the devil and his angels," Matt. xxv. 41; his followers, his dupes, his victims, among the former hosts of heaven and among the children of men, the apostate, corrupt, impenitent children of men. For it is the truth of God, and it ought to be told and believed and pondered and acted on, that all who die in their sins, dwell for ever in hell, with devils and damned spirits.

In their intolerable and eternal torments, these all glorify the power and justice, the holiness and truth of God. These are the attributes which lost spirits, whether of men or devils, illustrate; but these are not all the attributes of God. They are a part, but not all that is embraced in his "name." When that glorious Name is uttered they do come forth but not alone, not dissociated, not dissevered from the rest. All the attributes and all the perfections of God are collected and concentred and expressed in his Name. Holiness, justice, power, faithfulness, and truth are there, but along with them come trooping, other attributes, other perfections and such as accompany and promise salvation for penitent sinners, love, goodness, mercy, and grace. These all blend and shine in the redemption which is in Christ Jesus, our Lord, in the expressive Name of Jehovah, each with its proper and separate glory, all in undivided and united splendour, "with a far beaming blaze of majesty," as several colours in the rainbow, each distinguishable yet all harmonious, and each lending its separate ray to the one effulgent glory. The Name of God, therefore, comprehends all his adorable perfections, his love and grace, not less than his holiness and power; and when we are allowed to make our appeal to the Name of God for pardon, we are permitted to call to our help Jehovah himself, in the full glory of his being, in the entire circle of his attributes, in the unfathomable fulness of his nature, in his essential unity, in his tripersonal subsistence; not only as our Creator and Lord, but as our Redeemer and Saviour.

We are shut up to the gospel method of salvation, because we have the profound conviction, that God does demand and can demand nothing less than perfect holiness, and we are sensible that we can never attain it, that at no happy conjuncture of our lives can we hope to exhibit it, unless by the gospel method, the free and full forgiveness of our sins, the regeneration of our corrupt nature, the sanctification and renewal of all our faculties through the effectual working of the Holy Ghost; and as the answer of all the law's demands, the imputed righteousness of God himself, in the person of our atoning Saviour.

Let us, therefore, consider *the extent* of forgiveness. After what has been said on the import of the Name of God—the proper and only ground of the pardon of any sin; it is hoped, that we can see how any sin which man can commit may be forgiven, which does not by its nature preclude this plea. The greatness of the sin is really no bar, it may on the contrary be an argument, for its remission. We feel, that we are now treading on the perilous edge of a high truth, from which unreasonable and wicked men may fall into a yawning and infinite abyss; but it is a truth, nevertheless, and "let God be true and every man a liar." There is no sin, however great, which may not be pardoned "for his Name's sake," if it be repented of truly. The sin against the Holy Ghost is unpardonable, because it is of such a nature as to exclude repentance. It is to be constantly borne in mind that it was not on the ground that he had made a full confession, that the Psalmist implored and anticipated pardon.

The celebrated French deist, Rousseau, after making a shameful and sickening confession of his lies, and libertinism, and thefts, and manifold baseness, said that he would present this record of his life before the bar of God, in the confident anticipation, that a full confession would be accepted as a full atonement. But the pious Psalmist thought, and felt, and acted far otherwise. The greatness of the sin did not indeed cut off the hope of pardon ; but that hope was founded not on anything that he had done or could do, but simply on the Name of God, attended and attested by a godly sorrow for sin. The promises of Scripture to the true penitent, are such as may reasonably inspire hope in the chief of sinners. "The blood of Jesus Christ his Son cleanseth us from all sin, and if any man sin we have an advocate with the Father, Jesus Christ the righteous." The very design of our Lord's coming into the world is declared to have been, not to call the righteous, but sinners to repentance; and of old it was made a ground of accusation against him, that he received sinners and ate with them.

Rightly understood and proceeded on, however, this great truth, like every truth of Scripture, is not only innocent but highly profitable. What is repentance? and what is it to repent? It is to be truly sorry for sin, to wish it had never been committed, to hate it from the heart, to turn from it, to keep clear of it, as far as possible in all time to come; and all this is wrought in the heart of a sinner by the word and Spirit of God, and is attended by a trust in the mercy of God in Christ. The discriminating mark of a true penitent is, not that he avoids gross transgressions from the force of natural conscience, still less from respect to human opinion; but that he hates pollution, that he strives after holiness, that the personal consciousness of sin, whether known to another or not, is his grief and burden. Physical filth is not so intolerably loathsome to a person of purity and sensibility, as moral pollution to a real penitent, a servant and a saint of God. It is necessary not only to *confess* our sins, but to *mourn* for them, and not only to mourn for them, but to forsake them. Confession alone will not be followed by forgiveness, on the part of God, or by forsaking them on our part. There is no such mark of being a child of God by gracious adoption as the love of holiness, inward sighing, and striving after it. To be contented in the habit of sin, or with constantly recurring sins, as want of humility and fervency in our prayers, wandering of heart at the sacrament of the Lord's Supper, and the decay of brotherly love, is a sure sign, if not of the total want of grace, at least of its feebleness. If we truly love Christ himself, we shall love his people, his cause, his church, his work. The love of the Lord Jesus Christ is inconsistent with the love of sin, and as the one prevails, the other inevitably declines. So far as the permanent interests of virtue and morality are concerned, therefore, no matter how great a man's sins, if he really, truly, scripturally repent of them, there is no damage done to these high interests when he is forgiven. They are rather honoured and fortified. For if a man is a true penitent, he can not willingly commit these sins a second time, of which he has repented. David was a true penitent; did he murder another Uriah? Peter was a true penitent; did he deny his Divine Master after he had gone out and wept bitterly? Augustine was a true penitent; did he go back to his lies, and his libertinism, and to his old errors in philosophy and religion? Luther, Calvin, Zwingle, Knox, and Cranmer, were true penitents; did they return to the cruel and debasing superstitions of Rome?

Those men who are always repenting and always sinning, confessing before God and man that what they do is wrong, and still doing the same things over again, never have repented at all. Rightly understood then, not only is this doctrine consistent with the sacred interests of morality and piety, not only is it, in no way, repugnant to them, but in every way conducive, and altogether essential. If you wish to make a man a villain, a real, thorough, hardened, hopeless villain, all that you have to do is to let him commit one criminal and infamous offence, and then take away the hope of mercy, the possibility of his ever being restored to the respect and confidence of his fellows. Once make it plain to him that he must always be an outcast, no matter what he is, no matter what he does, and you have accomplished your object. You have made that man a reprobate for ever. You have broken the very spring of honour within. For true honour is based on an enlightened self-respect. You have poisoned the sweet fountain of humanity, and taught him to hate, and as much as he can to hurt mankind. You have razed to the very ground, the last foundation of virtue and real greatness of soul. You have demolished the whole structure of moral worth within him, and have not left a solitary peg, for a good principle, or purpose, or feeling to hang upon. This is the main reason why, when a woman once falls, her recovery is so difficult and rare; so close is the bond between a good reputation and a good character. But if you make it plain to the man that he may be restored to the respect of others by his repentance, established beyond all dispute by his change of conduct, the way is then open to him to be restored to his own self-respect, and so to recover his moral integrity. We may reasonably conclude therefore, that the forgiveness of great sins, on the condition of a true repentance—and none are ever forgiven on any other condition—is in no way detrimental to the high interests of morality, but on the contrary, their strong support and guard. That which shuts up the devils themselves to eternal infamy and anguish and rebellion is the certainty, that for them there is no forgiveness.

The pardon of the greatest sinner on such grounds and with such consequences, reflects peculiar honour on the divine perfections. His mercy then appears high as the heavens, equal to, yea greater than, the subtlety and malice and power of the devil, his enemy and ours. His wisdom and love in providing a Saviour then shine out in sovereign majesty, in surpassing splendour. The blood of Christ is then seen to be powerful and precious, infinitely exceeding in efficacy the blood of bulls and goats, though whole hecatombs were slain—vain sacrifice for human guilt!

We have seen how the general interests of truth and righteousness are affected by the exercise of grace in the forgiveness of great sins, and how the perfections of God stand related to it; now let us see what effect it will have on the sinner himself. This has been partially anticipated already, sufficiently to render it proper to dismiss the matter briefly, but not to pass it over altogether.

Fortunately for us, this is what the lawyers would call *a case ruled.* The judge has pronounced upon it. The highest court has explicitly and authoritatively decided it. When that sinful but penitent woman brought an alabaster-box full of precious ointment, and stood at his feet behind him weeping, and began to wash his feet with tears, and to wipe them with the hairs of her head, and kissed his feet and anointed them with the ointment; our Lord said, "Her sins which are many are forgiven, therefore she loved much, but to whom little is forgiven the same loveth little." Luke vii. 38–47.

There is therefore no bar in the way of the salvation of the greatest sinner but that which his own obstinate, self-destroying impenitence creates. The sacrifice of the Lord Jesus Christ upon the cross is of power to atone for the greatest and blackest iniquities. It cleanseth from *all* sin. It availed for the pardon of some who shed it, and it is of virtue sufficient to wash away your sins, horrible as they may have been! Let not the number or the malignity of your offences drive you away from that life-giving fountain, which hath been opened to the house of David and to the inhabitants of Jerusalem for sin and for uncleanness. Zech. xiii. 1. Jesus Christ "came not to call the righteous but sinners to repentance." Your sins are indeed numerous enough, heavy enough, aggravated enough, to crush your soul for ever, to sink you down to the lowest hell, but he is strong enough to bear the mighty load. They are weighty enough to crush a world, but he can bear them. He has borne them in his own body on the tree. Cast thy burden therefore upon him, and he will sustain thee. You must sink beneath the enormous load, unless the mighty God, the everlasting Father, the Prince of Peace, take it away. He has endured the full weight of the wrath of God, on the bitter cross, that they who believe in him might be exempt from the operation of law, and be graciously accepted in the

Beloved. Oppressed with sin, overwhelmed with grief and fear, offer then this prayer, if for the first time in all your life: "For thy name's sake pardon mine iniquity, O Lord, for it is great." In the whole Bible, you will not find a prayer better suited to you, a conscious and helpless sinner, unless it be the prayer of the publican, "God be merciful to me a sinner!"

It should ever be remembered, that no sin, however small it may seem to us, however small it may be comparatively considered, can be pardoned in any other way, on any other ground, than for the sake of what our blessed Lord has done and suffered for us. In relation to this point, two things are to be considered. The first is the deadly nature of the very least sin. The wages of sin, as sin, of any sin, is death. Though the sin committed or supposed, were the least conceivable, yet if unpardoned, God could punish it with nothing less than eternal death. Sin carries in it essentially, inevitably, always, the seed which when matured is death. The whole genesis of sin, moral and historical, in itself, in its working, and in its manifestation, is exhibited in the words of the apostle: "Lust when it hath conceived bringeth forth sin, and sin when it is finished bringeth forth death." Here then are the successive steps in the process—lust, sin, death.

The second thing to be considered is, that when a man has once committed the least sin against God, he may regret it, he may rue it, but he can make no atonement for it. No power or virtue can go forth from him to satisfy God. If it is ever covered, it must be by forgiveness. If it is ever forgiven, it must be, not for the sinner's sake, but for the sake of One not himself personally a sinner, but who has borne the penalty due to sin. The sinner himself can do absolutely nothing to satisfy law or justice, or to make amends for his offence against both. So that for the least sin we are shut up to a free forgiveness for the sake of Christ. It is evident, then, that in relation to the terms and to the method of pardon, all sinners are upon a perfect level. The way of salvation is the same for all. All that enter heaven must pass through one door, and that door is Christ; by one way, and that way is Christ; in the heartfelt reception of one truth, and that truth is Christ; in the inward appropriation of one life, and that life is Christ. The pride of the best, and the most moral, and conscientious, and sober, and respectable sinner, must come down to the thankful acceptance of a free pardon for the sake of Christ, or he can never be pardoned at all. God pardons no sin because it is little, but because the blood of Jesus Christ, the atoning Saviour, is precious, and his merit infinite.

It only remains for us to consider another truth nearly connected with this, or rather a different phase of this. As no sin, however great, will exclude us from the kingdom of heaven if we repent of it—none is so small as not to prove our everlasting perdition if unrepented of.

Our self-righteousness is one of the deepest and most delusive forms of our sinful corruption. Satan, too, knows full well, how to turn it to fatal account. It works in various ways according to the former history and existing circumstances of the sinner. When a man who hitherto has been cautious and careful, and so has been able to keep on good terms with his own conscience, is once overtaken in a great transgression, commits some gross iniquity as adultery, lying, drunkenness, theft, or forgery, the devil seeks to persuade him, and often with fatal success, to give up in despair, to surrender all hope of salvation, to abandon the fear of God, to deny the faith of the gospel, and depart from the path of piety for ever. This is a most critical juncture in his spiritual history. If Satan can prevail upon him to do this, his damnation slumbereth not. But if he will confess his sin to God and forsake it, and trust in his mercy in Christ, and so far as man is concerned, make such restitution as the nature of the case may admit of, there is hope for him still, —he may yet be forgiven and saved.

To sinners in other circumstances and of a different type, Satan presents a different temptation. He seeks to persuade them that it is unreasonable, that it is impossible that any should be consigned to the dark dungeons of everlasting despair, for such sins as they have committed. Now what I have to say to such, is, that the least sin you can commit is large enough to banish you from heaven, and sink you down to hell, unless it be truly repented of and fully pardoned. There is absolutely no way of escape for any sinner but by that new and living way which Christ opened for us through the veil, that is to say, his flesh. "Wherefore he is able to save them to the uttermost that come unto God by him, seeing he ever liveth to make intercession for them." Heb. vii. 25.

LECTURE XIV.

THE NEW HEAVENS AND THE NEW EARTH.

If we had a valuable estate in another country, should we not eagerly study any work relating to that country—describing its soil, climate, productions,—the character of the inhabitants, together with their occupations and enjoyments, and examine with the greater accuracy and diligence whatever might more particularly refer to the title, tenure, interests, and value of our own personal estate? Again, if we had a beloved friend or brother in that country, of whose history, and glory, and love, we wished to receive authentic intelligence, should we not ponder the volume containing the coveted information? To the Christian, heaven is that country, salvation that estate, the Bible that volume, and Christ that friend and brother.

The miser loves to retire, that he may feast his eyes with his "unsunned heaps"of perishable gold and silver. Why should not the heir of heaven itself, of a crown of righteousness that fadeth not away, of durable riches, gladly contemplate his precious and pleasant possessions—the inheritance of the saints in light?

If we delight in humble and holy meditation here, in believing and fervent prayer, in lively and spiritual praises to the God of our salvation, we may be assured that we have even now the taste and the temper which will render the services of the heavenly sanctuary congenial; when all sin shall be purged away, and we shall see God in his infinite glory, and serve him with ineffable delight!

One of the elements of interest and enjoyment in the heavenly state, will be wonder. God has crowded this world with brilliant and amazing objects, for the very purpose of kindling an expectation of greater wonders in the world to come. The broad sun sinking down in his tranquillity, the ocean, the mountains, the shifting and many-coloured clouds, the green sward, the happy and animated creatures—all excite a feeble interest in comparison with that which heaven will elicit; but they may serve to awaken within us the sense of God's power and glory, which will be so much heightened hereafter!

This present earth is temporary only. As man's body is mortal, and man dies because he is a sinner, so this tainted material universe, bearing the reflection, being the scene of sin, shall die after a fashion, shall disappear and give place ultimately to an untainted and everlasting materialism—the new heavens and the new earth, wherein dwelleth righteousness. It is sad to think, that the loveliest spots on this earth have been polluted by blood and by lust. The world endures, and is destined to endure, while the work of ingathering is going on, and is incomplete. It is a stage on which grand and successive acts of a divine drama are in progress. It is a temporary scaffolding which will be taken down when the spiritual temple has been reared and finished. Let the work of redemption, in all its glorious extent, be accomplished, let the last wandering and way-worn sinner be gathered into the fold and rest of God, and this will be the signal of the consummation of all things here below. The exulting and triumphant anthem with which ministering spirits shall celebrate the ingathering of the last of the sons of men who shall be the heir of salvation, may be regarded as the requiem of the world's destruction.

The closing chapters of divine revelation contain a magnificent description of the passing away of the old heavens and the old earth, and the glorious evolution of the new. The change from the dreariness and death of winter, to the cheerful green and bursting life of spring, is gradual. The change from the gloomy reign of night to the clear shining of the perfect day, when the morning is spread upon the mountains, is more rapid; but the morning-light does not transform or transfigure. It only illuminates and reveals. It shines upon the very same earth, that a few hours before was wrapped in the mantle of darkness. Here there is not a mere illumination, not even a glorious transfiguration, but a passing away of the one and a coming of the other, a removal and a substitution. Old things have passed away, behold all things have become new. There is now no more sea. The new Jerusalem, the redeemed, triumphant, and glorified church, comes down from God out of heaven. The marriage of the Lamb and his bride is about to be solemnized with the festive pomp and splendour, that befit the nuptials of the King's Son, and his unspotted and beloved bride. Then a mighty voice is heard, proclaiming the permanent abode of God with men, the ratification, the renewal, and the fulfilment of his gracious covenant. God himself shall be with them and be their God. Then will be fulfilled in its highest significance, our Saviour's intercessory prayer for his people—that they might be with him and behold his glory, the glory which he had with the Father before the world. John xvii. 5.

This is the prelude and the preparation. Then drawing nearer still, the Father's hand is stretched out, and touches and blesses them in their own persons. Before the original creation of man, the earth was prepared to receive him, and before the final blessedness of redeemed man, the new heavens and the new earth, his destined and glorious habitation, are fitted to receive him. Then the blessing comes upon him, the exceeding and eternal weight of glory, the honour and the happiness which flow from the immediate ministrations of the Father of mercies and God of all comfort. He himself wipes away all tears from their eyes, with the gentleness of parental love. He removes all occasion of remorse, disquiet, and anxiety. He buries in eternal oblivion the bitter memory of grief, save as it may purify and exalt the present sense of joy. And when these tears are wiped away, they are wiped away for ever. Not only the channel but the fountain of weeping is dried up. Now the reign of sorrow and of death hath ceased, and that of joy and of immortality commenced. Death himself is dead, and all his gloomy and hideous progeny, sorrow and crying, which is the outburst of sorrow, and pain, which is the eldest born of toil—these have all departed never more to return.

It might be imagined that the Christian heaven would be the point, to which the eyes of the men of every land and nation would be turned with an eager and incessant gaze. It is described as the everlasting abode of untroubled peace, where the wicked cease from troubling and the weary are at rest; as a sanctuary from which every thing profane and polluted, is rigorously shut out; as the region and the home of pure devotion and of perfect love; as the fitting palace of the everlasting King, in whose presence there is fulness of joy, and at whose right hand there are pleasures for ever more. The Bible does not give these descriptions, in order to excite a dream of Epicurean delight, but to animate us in the pursuit of a pure and perennial bliss; to assuage the sharp sense of present anguish: to disrobe this world of its fatal attractions; to raise us in spirit and in striving above what is seen and temporal, and engage our deepest thoughts and elicit our most strenuous efforts in the prosecution of objects unseen and eternal.

But does the revelation of this glorious rest animate us to incessant activity in the discharge of our earthly duties? Does the pleasant prospect which it unfolds render us insensible to the allurements of carnal pleasure? Do our thoughts habitually and delightedly turn to the serene enjoyments of our spiritual rest, when vexed with the countless cares of this present life? Do we find a readiness and a capacity within us to appropriate the exceeding great and precious promises, that God in his infinite mercy has made to the way-worn pilgrim? Do the sublime glimpses which revelation affords us of that house not made with hands, eternal in the heavens, inspire us with undaunted courage to contend with every enemy, and press at every hazard into the heavenly kingdom? It is true, we cannot see heaven with our bodily eyes, any more than we can see the glorious God of heaven. But as it is our duty to endure as seeing him who is invisible, so it is our part, not having seen this goodly possession, still to desire it and believe, though as yet we behold it not, that God hath prepared for us a heavenly city, and is not ashamed to be called our God.

The prospect of eternal glory should inflame our imaginations and our hearts. If the portals of heaven's sanctuary were thrown open to our enraptured gaze, and we could see the glowing ardours of the Seraphim, and listen to those harmonious notes that vibrate on the harps of gold, and fall prostrate with the hosts that bow in lowly reverence before "the throne and equipage of God's almightiness," we should be filled with a kindred worship and rapture and love.

It is not then merely a spiritual luxury, a feast of the imagination and the soul, to contemplate the final blessedness of this renovated scene, of paradise regained, the revealed glory of the new heavens and the new earth; it is not merely a transporting pleasure to think of heaven, to speak of heaven, to hear of heaven; but well and wisely considered, it is in the highest degree profitable. Such a contemplation, when scriptural and sober, will abound with moral lessons addressed to the conscience, it will lend most effectual aid to the daily discipline of our hearts and lives, while it will animate the soul with the most delightful prospects, and stimulate Christian zeal and spiritual diligence with the most attractive and holy visions—visions of a beauty far more beauteous, of a glory far more glorious, than ever burst upon the eye or beamed upon the heart of mortal man. It is to us a token and a sample of the unimaginable fruitfulness of the promised land, like the grapes of Eshcol. It is a premonition of the coming bliss, like the perfumed gales that blow far off from the Spice Islands, and encourage the tempest-tost mariner in his sore conflict with the rocks and waves.

The gracious design of these glorious revelations, is to comfort afflicted believers under the hard pressure of earthly ills, to cast the light of promise and of hope over the deep darkness of God's dispensations toward them now, to make them joyful in all tribulations, and instant in prayer, "knowing in themselves that they have in heaven a better and an enduring substance." Heb. x. 34.

It is a foolish and wicked abuse for carnal persons, whether in the church or out of the church, to take the children's bread; to appropriate the cheer, the wine, and oil, and pleasant fruits, the mountains of myrrh and hills of frankincense, the milk and honey, the fountains and orchards, which God hath ordained for the refreshment and delight of his fainting children; of such as are poor in spirit, and hunger and thirst after righteousness, and desire no earthly promotion, no natural joy, so much as that their souls may drink abundantly from the fountain of goodness, the well of living waters, and that they may be filled, not with carnal delights and treasures, but with that holy peace which springs from the indwelling of the Spirit of God, and passeth all understanding.

There are three worlds of which we read in Scripture: this world, and heaven, and hell. Of this world alone have we any direct, sensible, personal experience or knowledge now. All that we do know or that we can know of heaven and hell, while we continue in the flesh, must be derived from revelation.

This world is, we know, a mixed, uncertain, changeful, transient state—a place of perpetual conflict between light and darkness, good and evil. Hell is a place of unmixed evil and wretchedness, unimaginable and everlasting woe. Heaven is a place of pure and perfect blessedness, of ineffable glory and delight.

Even this present evil world is beautiful; though the abode of birds and beasts, of evil beasts and unclean birds, and hissing, hideous snakes, and foul and abominable creeping things; though it is under the curse of God and under the dominion of sin, still, it is in many things a beautiful world. In the Greek tongue it has its name thence—*Κοσμος*, beauty, arrangement, order, harmony, ornament, honour, referring to the unnumbered prints of the Creator's beauty, still plainly to be seen upon it. And if this earth, defiled by sin, is so beautiful, what will the new heavens and the new earth be? In them the goodness of God will have supreme dominion and unimpeded flow; its infinite riches will be poured forth in infinite profusion of beauty and joy. If the earth is robed with flowers, and laced with shining streams, and girdled with glorious mountains, and ramparted with the everlasting hills, and the munitions of rocks, and watered with streams from above and from below, and her dark places enriched with precious stones, with the lustre of pearls, and diamonds, and rubies; if even the sands of the seas and the rivers are all ablaze with corals, and gems, and gold, if fragrant and beautiful blossoms grow wild and plentiful on every tree; and the firmament overhead is crowned with a kingly diadem of stars, what must the new heavens and the new earth be?

Heaven is set forth to us in Scripture under the emblem of a marriage feast; but to take away all gross conceptions, we are told that the glorified bodies of the risen saints will be spiritual. The pleasures of seeing and hearing, of all sensible delights the most refined and pure, and not unmixed with reason—delights of which the brutes appear to have no sense or relish, are used to represent the blessedness of the heavenly state to our apprehension—thrones, palms, crowns, white raiment, bursts of choral melody, and songs of celestial gladness. Rev. vii. 13–17. These images, we know, are figurative, but they must be adapted to set forth the fundamental spiritual truth, and convey it with superior force and vividness to us—or "men who wrote as they were moved by the Holy Ghost," would not have selected and employed them.

All our conceptions of heavenly things must, of necessity, be conditioned by those sensible objects wherewith we are now surrounded. Hence, its happiness and glory are represented as consisting very much in the absence of sensible evils, all of which are in fact the fruits of sin. Thus it is affirmed that "God shall wipe away all tears from the eyes" of the redeemed. What image could be more tender and touching? What more expressive of a father's sympathy? The sorrows of the saints shall cease, not by necessity of nature, but by the grace of their heavenly Father. With soft and gentle hand he will wipe away the falling tear, and then a smile of gratitude and gladness shall spread over the happy faces of his favoured children—the voice of weeping be heard no more, nor the spectacle of tears be seen again. The saints will then be done with their sorrows for ever. All men, often the best men, experience bitter sorrows here. Those clothed in white raiment, which is the righteousness of the saints, with palms of victory in their hands, have come up out of great tribulation. Out of dark valleys, out of lowly depths, they go up to the mountain of the Lord's house, the Mount Zion of God. Here the living stones of the heavenly temple are quarried, and cut, and shaped, and fitted, to their predestined and proper place, and according to the beautiful accommodation of one of our admirable old Puritan divines,* as the stones that were to enter into the typical temple of Solomon, were hewn and chiselled afar off, so that no sound of the hammer was heard in the holy and beautiful house

* Bates, to whom I am indebted for several valuable thoughts in this chapter.

of Jehovah; so the true children of the Most High, the living stones of the heavenly temple, are hewn by sorrows here, and then assume their places, polished after the similitude of a palace, in the true tabernacle which the Lord pitched, and not man—the celestial temple, pervaded by uncreated light, not that of the sun or the moon, but of the Lamb, resounding through all its vast chambers, and vaulted dome, and pillared aisles, not with such melody as is heard on earth, but with the sweet and holy chants of angel-voices, harping on their harps of gold, to responsive choirs of blood-bought, happy souls, ascribing salvation to the Lamb that was slain.

Then there shall be no more death. Death is now the king of terrors, the consummation and climax of earthly ills, in the apprehension of mankind. There is nothing which they dread so much, and if they are not Christians, so justly; for it cuts them off from every earthly blessing and consigns them to everlasting woe. But then death for ourselves or our dear friends is felt and feared no more. Now we dwell in the region and shadow of death, in a world in which death reigns naturally over every son and daughter of Adam. But that is the land of life and truly the land of the living. For there Christ who is, in the supremest sense, *the Life*, lives and reigns in all and over all. Christ himself, the original, full, perennial, over-flowing fountain of life, in the midst of the paradise of God, and as the four streams watered and made fruitful and bright and glad, the remotest borders of the earthly Eden. So this heavenly fountain, this true life, this anointed Saviour, our Lord and Saviour Jesus Christ, who is himself the essential and eternal life, will flow forth in living streams of blessing and grace, of salvation and glory, over all the realms and provinces of the new heavens and the new earth.

The destruction of death, which is the essence and issue of all other evils, ensures the termination of all the maladies which now afflict the body. How many drag a crazy, creaking, crumbling body, all their lives! Now we are frail, vulnerable, exposed to a whole cohort of fevers, and to accidents and injuries without number or name. There it will not be so. Christ shall bestow on us a body as it shall please him, a better body and a more beautiful body than Adam's was in its first creation. His was a natural body. He had innocent infirmities. Ours will be a spiritual and glorious body, like that of Christ in heaven. The unbelieving scribes stumbled at this doctrine when our Lord taught it, not knowing the Scriptures, nor the power of God. But why should we stumble at it? Is any thing naturally impossible to omnipotence? Cannot God give us a spiritual body just as easily as he gave us a natural body? The superior excellence of the work presents no difficulty to a divine Architect—an almighty Creator.

Then all mental griefs, which are the most tormenting and terrible, will be ended, and the happiness of the soul will be perfect, for it will be akin to that of the blessed God himself. What is the nature of the happiness of God, and whence does it arise? It is a holy and supreme blessedness, and it arises from the full knowledge and enjoyment of his own infinite perfections. The happiness of the saints in glory will spring from the same inexhaustible source. The Lord is their portion. The author of their blessedness, the object of their adoration, is the supreme God in his manifested glory. The most comprehensive faculties of the soul, are the understanding and the will including the affections. How suitable a portion, this infinite Being to the soul of man!

The affections of man are a most sacred and priceless gift. By these he communes with his fellows and with his God. By these his heart softens at the recollection of the dead, and the strong man weeps like a little child. By these his intellect is prompted and fed, and to these it is mainly subservient.

There is an inherent difference between the righteous and the wicked affections. A man whose mind is disordered, uneasy, embittered, will turn any the most indifferent and familiar action into matter of harsh censure and clamorous complaint. He will make himself and every one around him unhappy, by his sensitive and suspicious disposition, his sulky and querulous behaviour. His acid and abominable temper will turn every thing to sorrow; especially, and by a just judgment of God, his own evil heart. A man whose soul is serene and loving and peaceful, will easily turn aside every untoward and provoking incident, so that its very quality shall seem changed. Hence the necessity of sanctification to heaven. Well, therefore, may we beg of God, to cast out all uncleanness, and all wrath and strife and envying, from our hearts. We know from our own experience, that to be happy we must be good; and that well-disposed affections are the chief sources of true and lasting enjoyment. God has so constituted us, that we cannot be wicked without being wretched. Every blow inflicted on another recoils on ourselves. According to the striking oriental fiction, mentioned by Southey, in which a man has a serpent growing from between his shoulders, and finds to his horror that it is a part of himself, and every blow that falls on the serpent falls on himself.

In fixing our affections upon God as their proper object, the perfection and blessedness of our spiritual nature will be attained. With regard to all men, to a lamentable extent, the forces and faculties of the soul, spiritual in their principle and nature, are sensual in respect both to their objects and application. Hence our confusion, disappointment, sorrow, and disgust. Hence weariness of life attended by the dread of death, a feeling of misspent labour and unsatisfied desire.

In heaven, the noblest faculties of our spiritual nature will be directed toward a spiritual and perfect object. They will be fixed on the everlasting God with ever-increasing wonder and delight. They will grow by what they gaze on. They will grow by what they feed on. Each added ray from that all-glorious orb, will strengthen and sharpen the spiritual organ. The powers of the soul will first be so purged and invigorated, as to be prepared for heaven; for now we could not see God and live; now we could not breathe in that pure air. There we shall be attempered to it, and rejoice in it, as in our native element. We shall move with immortal vigour and delight, amid scenes of celestial majesty and splendour. The nation of the saved will grow in power, in knowledge, in dignity, and in blessedness, throughout eternal ages. Now we can behold God only as his image is reflected in his works, and expressed in his word, as in a glass darkly; then, we shall be admitted to the immediate intuition of his glory, the unveiled manifestation of his adorable person. God is a Spirit, therefore for ever invisible to the eye of sense; and as he is an infinite Spirit, and we are finite, we shall never be able to find him out to perfection. We shall, indeed, behold him after a more wonderful and excellent manner, for we shall not only be with him, but be like him, for we shall see him as he is.

The necessity of a spiritual regeneration may be argued and enforced from a consideration of the nature and sources of the happiness of the saints in light. These joys are not sensual, or such as sensual persons are capable of tasting, but spiritual and holy. Without holiness no man shall see the Lord. Into the heavenly city nothing can enter that defileth. Without are dogs, and whoremongers, and adulterers, and drunkards, and all liars. Ye must be born again—from above, to partake of the divine delights of the new heavens and the new earth. They consist in a soul purified from all sinful dregs and defilements, and completely filled with the knowledge and fitted to the worship of the infinite and ever blessed God. Its supreme blessedness consists in the plenary enjoyments of God, and in conscious fellowship with his faithful servants in their fervent and lofty praises. Without love we could not be happy in heaven. The love of God is the essential character of the heavenly city. Love is the cement that binds together heavenly minds. It is the gravitating law of the celestial sphere, which keeps them all in their proper orbits, and causes them to revolve in eternal harmony and gladness, around the great central Luminary—the Sun of Righteousness, the ornament and glory of the heavenly world—the Lord Jesus Christ, our most gracious Redeemer.

It will make the joys of heaven the sweeter, to enter upon them after the troubles of this life—to pass from the confusion, the darkness, the disappointment, and the turmoil of earth, to the harmony, the peace, the rest, the light, and the joy of heaven! This idea of bliss in contrast with previous privation or positive woe, and of the one as a preparation as well as a precursor of the other, is plainly held out to us in the images under which the blessedness of the righteous is at once veiled and revealed in the Scriptures. It is an untroubled and eternal Sabbatism, a rest that remaineth to the people of God. We feel our earthly Sabbaths all the more sacred and delightful, for the strifes, and secularities, and labours of the six preceding days. And we shall find our heavenly rest all the more welcome and dear, for the pains, and perils, and wanderings of earth; when we shall pass from earth to heaven, through death to life, from the gloom of the grave to that glorious city, where they have no need of the sun, neither of the moon to shine in it: for the glory of God doth lighten it, and the Lamb is the light thereof.

It is a pleasure to him that hath been long tossed upon the sea, to gain the haven of repose; a pleasure to him that hath borne the strength and fury of battle, to lie down in the lap of peace; a pleasure to him who hath endured the burden and heat of the day, to see the long-descending shadows of evening falling around him. And even to the marvellous delights of the heavenly Canaan will it add another and a higher zest, to taste them after hungering in the wilderness, after wandering in the desert.

www.ingramcontent.com/pod-product-compliance
Lightning Source LLC
LaVergne TN
LVHW010212110826
845151LV00004B/1061

* 9 7 8 1 4 2 5 5 2 8 7 8 2 *